[H.A.S.C. No. 114–141]

NATIONAL SECURITY SPACE: 21ST CENTURY CHALLENGES, 20TH CENTURY ORGANIZATION

HEARING

BEFORE THE

SUBCOMMITTEE ON STRATEGIC FORCES

OF THE

COMMITTEE ON ARMED SERVICES
HOUSE OF REPRESENTATIVES

ONE HUNDRED FOURTEENTH CONGRESS

SECOND SESSION

HEARING HELD
SEPTEMBER 27, 2016

U.S. GOVERNMENT PUBLISHING OFFICE

22–459   WASHINGTON : 2017

For sale by the Superintendent of Documents, U.S. Government Publishing Office
Internet: bookstore.gpo.gov   Phone: toll free (866) 512–1800; DC area (202) 512–1800
Fax: (202) 512–2104   Mail: Stop IDCC, Washington, DC 20402–0001

SUBCOMMITTEE ON STRATEGIC FORCES

MIKE ROGERS, Alabama, *Chairman*

TRENT FRANKS, Arizona
DOUG LAMBORN, Colorado, *Vice Chair*
MIKE COFFMAN, Colorado
MO BROOKS, Alabama
JIM BRIDENSTINE, Oklahoma
J. RANDY FORBES, Virginia
ROB BISHOP, Utah
MICHAEL R. TURNER, Ohio
JOHN FLEMING, Louisiana

JIM COOPER, Tennessee
LORETTA SANCHEZ, California
RICK LARSEN, Washington
JOHN GARAMENDI, California
BRAD ASHFORD, Nebraska
PETE AGUILAR, California
(Vacancy)

STEVE KITAY, *Professional Staff Member*
LEONOR TOMERO, *Counsel*
MIKE GANCIO, *Clerk*

(II)

CONTENTS

Page

STATEMENTS PRESENTED BY MEMBERS OF CONGRESS

Rogers, Hon. Mike, a Representative from Alabama, Chairman, Subcommittee on Strategic Forces 1

WITNESSES

Ellis, ADM James O., Jr., USN (Ret.), Former Commander, U.S. Strategic Command 5

Faga, Martin C., Former Director, National Renaissance Office, Former Assistant Secretary of the Air Force for Space 7

Hamre, Dr. John J., Former Deputy Secretary of Defense 4

APPENDIX

PREPARED STATEMENTS:

    Cooper, Hon. Jim, a Representative from Tennessee, Ranking Member, Subcommittee on Strategic Forces 38

    Ellis, ADM James O., Jr. 47

    Faga, Martin C. 58

    Hamre, Dr. John J. 39

    Rogers, Hon. Mike 35

DOCUMENTS SUBMITTED FOR THE RECORD:

    GAO chart, "Finding 1: DOD Space Acquisitions, Management, and Oversight Are Fragmented Across Approximately 60 Stakeholders" 69

WITNESS RESPONSES TO QUESTIONS ASKED DURING THE HEARING:

    [There were no Questions submitted during the hearing.]

QUESTIONS SUBMITTED BY MEMBERS POST HEARING:

    Mr. Cooper 79

    Mr. Coffman 84

    Mr. Lamborn 80

    Mr. Rogers 73

NATIONAL SECURITY SPACE: 21ST CENTURY CHALLENGES, 20TH CENTURY ORGANIZATION

HOUSE OF REPRESENTATIVES,
COMMITTEE ON ARMED SERVICES,
SUBCOMMITTEE ON STRATEGIC FORCES,
Washington, DC, Tuesday, September 27, 2016.

The subcommittee met, pursuant to call, at 2:59 p.m., in room 2118, Rayburn House Office Building, Hon. Mike Rogers (chairman of the subcommittee) presiding.

OPENING STATEMENT OF HON. MIKE ROGERS, A REPRESENTATIVE FROM ALABAMA, CHAIRMAN, SUBCOMMITTEE ON STRATEGIC FORCES

Mr. ROGERS. Good afternoon. I want to welcome everyone to the Strategic Forces Subcommittee's hearing on "National Security Space: 21st Century Challenges, 20th Century Organization."

We are honored to have a very distinguished panel of expert witnesses today. We have Dr. John Hamre, former Deputy Secretary of Defense; Retired Admiral James Ellis, former commander of U.S. STRAT Command—Strategic Command—the acronyms around here are just getting to me; Mr. Martin Faga, former director of the National Reconnaissance Office and Assistant Secretary of the Air Force for Space.

Dr. Hamre, you are respected on both sides of the political aisle and known to be a wise and thoughtful leader on defense issues. And I am aware that you have been studying space issues with a group of experts for some time. And I am grateful to see you engaging in this very important subject.

Admiral Ellis, you and Mr. Faga, your leadership in the national security space during your careers, as well as your recent cochairing of the National Academies study on Space Defense and Protection, will provide this committee a very informed view regarding today's issues.

So why are we here today? I would like to start with a quote. "It is not sufficient to have just resources, dollars and weapon systems. We must also have an organization which will allow us to develop the proper strategy, necessary planning and the full warfighting capability. We do not have this adequate organization structure today."

"We have made improvements, but those improvements have only been made at the margin. We need to do much more to be able to fight in today's environment that will require the concerted efforts for all four services."

"The services can't operate alone. We are basically a committee system. Committees are very good at deliberative process, but they are notoriously poor in trying to run things," closed quote.

This statement rings true for today's hearing. In fact, those words were spoken in this very same hearing room by a person sitting in this very same seat as our witnesses are sitting today.

However, the statement was made by a witness in February of 1982. The witness was the Chairman of the Joint Chiefs of Staff, Air Force General David Jones, speaking about the organization of the Joint Staff. The statement General Jones made took great courage and upset many people in the Department of Defense at the time.

Organizational change is hard, and unfortunately, many people take it personally. However, General Jones' candor with Congress led to one of the most sweeping, greatly needed reforms of the DOD [Department of Defense], the Goldwater-Nichols Department of Defense Reorganization Act of 1986.

Just as General Jones had the courage to talk honestly with this committee, I commend the witnesses today who have had the courage to discuss the challenges of the posture and organization of our national security space activities.

No one in this room needs to be convinced of the importance of space to national security. Space allows our warfighters to project power across the globe and to keep our homeland safe. Unfortunately, potential adversaries have recognized this, and they are developing weapons to take away the advantages that we have built into space.

There is a fundamental question before us today. Is the Department of Defense strategically postured to effectively respond to these threats and to prioritize the changed space domain over the long term? It is all too clear that we are not.

There is no clear leadership of the military space domain below the Secretary of Defense. Yes, there is an adviser, councils, chiefs, directors, and even commanders. As the GAO [Government Accountability Office] states, "DOD space leadership responsibilities are fragmented," closed quote.

While we certainly have great leaders within the space enterprise, the structure is set up such that far too many people are able to say no without the consequence for the delay and the costs they create. Those responsible for the organizing, training, equipping, and operational missions in the national security space are not actually in charge.

As General Hyten told the Senate Armed Services Committee in his confirmation hearing last week, "We are moving much slower in certain areas than our adversaries. We need our industry and our acquisition process to move faster," closed quote. I agree with General Hyten that we need to move faster.

However, I am concerned with the performance I am seeing today. For example, the GPS [Global Positioning System] next-generation ground system program is currently going through the Nunn-McCurdy breach for massive cost overruns, including a delay of operational capability that is 5 years beyond when it was originally planned.

And I would like to talk about the Air Force mismanagement of the weather satellite program, but I don't wanna get spitting mad in front of everybody today. Unfortunately, this is not a single point case, and it raises questions on the current enterprise's ability to deliver the next-generation space system to address the threat we face.

Separately, the military space activities are managed within conflicting priorities of each of the armed services. Many resisted the views of the airpower visionaries, such as Brigadier General Billy Mitchell and General Henry "Hap" Arnold, to have an independent Air Force. However, very few will argue today of the wisdom of their vision.

We have the best military and civilian space professionals, alongside the most talented industry in the world. I believe the question is not of their ability, but rather what tools, structures, incentives, and responsibilities and authority we need to give them to succeed. Put it another way, even the best leaders can't succeed with a failed system.

For those that shy away from reform, I ask if it is better to wait for a crisis to motivate those to change, or to instead build a better system in a thoughtful and a deliberate manner in order to avert such a crisis in the future. Dr. Hamre foreshadows in his statement for the record, "Space systems will be attacked," closed quote.

The 9/11 Commission noted that we had all the information and people we needed to prevent the day's events. We suffered from a "failure of imagination," closed quote. We must resist temptation of bureaucrats to wait for a disaster to fix this known failure. We must expect better. This committee will.

This hearing is the start of a focused oversight that we will conduct on this important topic. I anticipate it will lead to major reform in the Fiscal Year 2018 National Defense Authorization Act.

I thank the witnesses again for being with us today. I am looking forward to your testimony.

I now recognize my friend and colleague from Tennessee, Mr. Cooper, for any opening statement he may have.

[The prepared statement of Mr. Rogers can be found in the Appendix on page 35.]

Mr. COOPER. Thank you, Mr. Chairman, and welcome to the witnesses. I am happy to join the chairman in this effort. I am glad that we have got, once again, the coveted mid-afternoon hearing spot.

[Laughter.]

Not everyone is able to achieve that in the way we have.

[Laughter.]

But I would just ask unanimous consent my opening statement be inserted for the record. I look forward to the testimony of the three wise men here.

[The prepared statement of Mr. Cooper can be found in the Appendix on page 38.]

Mr. ROGERS. I now will recognize the witnesses and I ask—first of all, thank you for being here. Thank you for the time it takes to prepare your statements for this hearing and to present your testimony. It is very valuable in assisting us in trying to develop the policy that is so sorely needed in the subject matter area.

And with that, we will start with Dr. Hamre. You are recognized for 5 minutes to summarize your statement. And I would say for—all statements will be admitted in total for the record, so you can summarize, if you want to, or you can read it, either way. With that, Dr. Hamre, you are recognized.

STATEMENT OF DR. JOHN J. HAMRE, FORMER DEPUTY SECRETARY OF DEFENSE

Dr. HAMRE. Mr. Chairman, thank you. Mr. Cooper, thank you. I know every witness comes and says how grateful they are to be here and how grateful we are for your leadership. I really do think you are doing an essential service right now.

You know, we have been drifting for 8 years, maybe 10 years, with the knowledge that our space systems are deeply vulnerable, and we have not acted in any way in a manner that is commensurate with the nature of the threat we face. So I really am grateful that you are willing to take the lead here for the Congress, because this is crucial.

I do have a statement, and I normally would, you know, go through it. I am not going to do that, if I may, because I know you have had a chance to look at it. I would like to say, you know, the Department does have pockets of real excellence in space. And you see the superb machines that we have built over time. I mean, these are marvels, the things we have done.

And there are people that go to work every day with astounding dedication, you know, really working hard. But somehow, in a macro sense, we are failing to see what is obvious now to us, that our opponents understand quite well what they could do to change our entire posture. And we are not responding in a very effective way.

And I ask myself why? Why is it that, when it is so obvious what is happening, why isn't that we have been able to respond?

And, you know, the one thing I have done is spend a lot of time thinking about organization in the Department of Defense. And there is no perfect way to organize the Department of Defense. It is such a vast enterprise. And I will say my testimony, it is about moats and bridges.

I mean it. When you create an institution, the first thing that institution does is dig a moat around itself to protect itself bureaucratically. And it is up to then the Secretary to find ways to get bridges, you know, and drawbridges and hopefully they are down all the time, you know, where we can get them working together. And we are failing here on this.

We do have mighty moats separating things, but we are not bringing the whole together effectively. There are three crucial circles. If you think of a Venn diagram, they shouldn't be perfectly overlapped. There is only one place where these three circles overlapped in the building, and that is with the Secretary.

But you have an organizing principle, the title 10 authority. You recruit people, you train them, you build facilities for them, you know, you give them equipment, et cetera. So you have got a title 10 organizing principle. You have got an operational response of people that go to work every day to execute a military mission.

And then the third circle is the strategic guidance. What are we doing? Those three are not in alignment in an effective way in the Department. And they haven't been in in an effective way for probably 20 years.

That is, I will hope with your work you help bring a focus, how to bring those into proper alignment. We do have people that are going to work every day operating the satellites. We do have people who are going today building things, although I would say our recent performance has been disappointing compared to what it could have been and what it was in the past.

We have, again, pockets of excellence. NRO [National Reconnaissance Office] is a pocket of excellence. But we are not uniformly excellent. I would say the piece that is missing is leadership. Now, that is the purpose of your hearing today, and I indicate in my lit- tle testimony, you know, there are four broad things you could do. You could create a fifth service, big mighty moat, very hard to build bridges. You could create an analog to the Missile Defense Agency with space. That takes care of the title 10 authority. That takes care of the operational authority. It doesn't solve the leadership question.

You could restore the stature of the Space Command, make it a four-star equivalent combatant commander, along with the Strategic Command. That is the easiest thing to do.

You could give it SOCOM [Special Operations Command]-like authorities, you know, where it buys things—so you could again solve it. You are still not solving the leadership question.

And then a fourth option is you create kind of a parallel to the Navy and the Marine Corps, where it is the Department of the Navy. You have a Department of Air Force, but you have got a separate service that is worrying about space.

All of these are options. None of them still get at this core question of leadership at the top. And I know that the Department, or recently, they have tried to solve this by making the Secretary of the Air Force kind of the senior person. It is just not providing the leadership that we need as a nation.

Let me stop at that, and we will come back and talk to it. My time is out, sir. Thank you.

[The prepared statement of Dr. Hamre can be found in the Appendix on page 39.]

Mr. ROGERS. Thank you.

Admiral Ellis, you are recognized for 5 minutes.

STATEMENT OF ADM JAMES O. ELLIS, JR., USN (RET.), FORMER COMMANDER, U.S. STRATEGIC COMMAND

Admiral ELLIS. [Inaudible] for your calling this hearing today, and I am pleased to appear before it with my distinguished colleagues. As you mentioned, Marty Faga and I had the privilege of co-chairing a study over the last year and a half related to national security space protection and defense.

And as I noted in my prepared testimony, that addressed technological, policy, and strategic issues. It did not address organizational findings and recommendations. And I appear at the invitation of the subcommittee to present my personal views on these critical issues, not those of other study participants or the National Academy.

In my few minutes of opening remarks, I want to touch on a couple of areas that I think are essential to successfully addressing this urgent national security need. They touch, bin largely into seven specific areas that, based on my long-ago naval background and, perhaps, in a too-cute pun I call the seven C's, because each of them begin with "C."

And the first of them is commitment. We are facing a serious multifaceted threat to our use of space in support of our national security. And as Dr. Hamre has noted, the threat to our space assets has been emerging over two decades at an increasing rate, and our response to challenges identified long ago has been too slow.

We now understand that mitigation of the threat and creating resilience in our space systems will require a focused effort over many years by many organizations. There is not a one-and-done so- lution. Whatever changes we make, be they policy, strategy, oper- ational, technical, or organizational, must be rapid, flexible, effi- cient, and effective, and we must be committed to the task.

The second "C" is capabilities, as you have noted. It is no secret that in the realm of national security space we are not where we need to be. We need enhanced and focused intelligence, dramati- cally improved space situational awareness, improved technical ca- pabilities, and tactical tools made readily available to those we hold responsible every day for space security.

We need to make resilience a specified requirement in all ele- ments of our systems, and understand both that not all threats to our space systems are in space and not all countermeasures or re- sponses are on orbit.

Finally, and perhaps most importantly, we need better tools to analyze our space-related critical infrastructure so that we under- stand where the risk is greatest and the need most urgent so as to appropriately prioritize allocation of resources to get the most improvement in the shortest period of time.

The third "C" is competence. We must effectively integrate na- tional security space policy and strategy with procurement and operational capabilities. Neither can function well without the other. Diffused capabilities are often necessary to meet the varied needs of warfighters, but there must be consistency of policy and strategy and mechanisms for sharing technological innovation, pro- curement efficiencies, and best practices.

I fear bureaucracies as much as anyone, but Admiral Hyman Rickover was fond of saying, "If everyone is responsible, no one is responsible." There must be a leader, a champion for national secu- rity space at a level that cannot be ignored.

The fourth "C" is credibility. Some use the word competence and credibility interchangeably. In my view, they are not the same at all. Competence is what you are, but credibility is what people think you are.

Our national credibility in addressing national security space is shaped both by our policy and our strategy. I believe, as President Kennedy did, that conflict in space is not necessarily inevitable. By our policies and leadership, we can deal with the space environ- ment we have while shaping the environment we want.

A clear and credible national space strategy is essential to defining deterrent concepts appropriate for the space environment. As I sometimes note, tactical energy in a strategic vacuum is a recipe for disaster.

The fifth "C" is communication. Clear and unambiguous communication is essential to success in this effort. Externally, the tone and tenor of the conversation must be balanced and appropriate, but they must also be realistic in both reassuring allies and deterring adversaries.

As a nation we must be clear as to what we stand for in space and what we will not stand for. Internal communication is also critical to shared understanding among those many entities in the interagency process.

The sixth "C" is collaboration. Just as space can be seen as a newer version of the maritime global commons, addressing the security challenges demands a collective and international approach. Internationally, we must lead and shape not a coalition of the willing, but a coalition of the ready, willing, and able.

This cannot be seen as a United States effort alone. It must be viewed as what it is, a shared effort for the benefit and security of all humankind. Domestically, the commercial space sector in all its diversity must be a real partner in the operational and policy effort along with NASA [National Aeronautics and Space Administration] and NOAA [National Oceanic and Atmospheric Administration]. In fairness, we have seen nascent efforts in this area, but there is still much to be done.

The seventh "C" is courage, as you noted earlier, Mr. Chairman. Effectively addressing the national security space challenges will require organizational and individual courage. We often say that change is hard, but the reality is that things change all the time. In my view, it is the rate and acceleration of change that is hard. In engineering terms, the first and second derivative.

Creating an appropriate national security space architecture, improved analytical capabilities, enhanced capabilities, greater robustness, essential resilience, and real deterrence will require a sustained effort and real and effective change.

I thank you and look forward to your questions.

[The prepared statement of Admiral Ellis can be found in the Appendix on page 47.]

Mr. ROGERS. Thank you, Admiral.

Mr. Faga, you are recognized for 5 minutes.

STATEMENT OF MARTIN C. FAGA, FORMER DIRECTOR, NATIONAL RENAISSANCE OFFICE, FORMER ASSISTANT SECRETARY OF THE AIR FORCE FOR SPACE

Mr. FAGA. Thank you, Mr. Chairman and thank you. The clock is still counting. Thanks for the invitation to appear here today. I knew that my colleagues were going to develop the organizational issues that you raised, so I would like to develop it from the perspective of acquisition, where I am most expert and which is a key component of the challenges that confront us.

During the conduct of the NRC [National Research Council] study, we recognized that acquisition has to be more flexible and far faster than it is today. The current times an analysis of alternatives [AOA] typically takes 2 years. At the end of that time, it is commonly recommended that we continue on the same course.

General Hyten recently noted that when he asked the authors of a recent AOA why they had recommended the status quo, they replied that they had received no requirements for resilience, so they didn't know how to treat it. Now that isn't a very desirable answer, but it is understandable. The combat commanders don't yet know how to answer that question.

Our space programs are accomplished by program managers [PMs]. They are my most admired people. In its recent report on defense space acquisitions, the GAO noted that for some programs, PMs are reviewed by 56 organizations at 8 levels above them. Needless to say, these long processes consume months and much of the time and energy of the program manager.

In its report the GAO also stated, "By contrast the NRO's processes appear more streamlined than DOD's." Why is that? There are a number of reasons. The NRO has a relatively narrow mission and its high priority is widely acknowledged. The NRO is a joint activity of the DNI [Director of National Intelligence] and the Secretary of Defense, and the director reports to them through a very short reporting chain.

The NRO can fully engage in the budget process of which it is a part. I gave many more reasons in my written testimony that we can talk about later, if you wish.

In addition to DOD and NRO space activities, there is a third element, commercial space systems with national security application. Today this is primarily satellite imaging and satellite communications [SATCOM]. The DOD buys lots of satellite communications, but usually with short-term contracts.

For years, SATCOM operators have pushed the government to engage in longer term arrangements that would encourage and guide investments. There is an example of where the government did exactly that.

NGA [National Geospatial-Intelligence Agency] has a 10-year fixed price contract with DigitalGlobe to deliver imagery as a service. This meant that DigitalGlobe capitalized the satellites, that is they raised the money, had them built, launched them, and operates them. NGA has substantial tasking rights and gets a large portion of the daily take, all for an annual fee.

I will close by offering just a few thoughts on organizations. Ideas have been put forth for many years of ways to organize space more effectively, to put one person in charge, and to streamline. We do need to remember that acquisition of national space systems is carried out almost entirely by three organizations: Air Force Space and Missile Systems Center, NRO, and Navy Space and Naval Warfare Systems Command.

All are relatively small, on the scale of military organizations, and capable organizations that work effectively on behalf of their users. Operations are carried out by Air Force Space Command and smaller Navy and Army commands. The problem they all have to deal with is those many levels in organizations above them that interact with every decision that they make.

One common prescription is to establish a very senior position charged to pull all of this together. I worry that instead of solving the problem, we simply increase 56 to 57, and I have seen that before. Moreover, and the most important thing I will say today, in my experience, the most important thing is to keep the acquisition process tightly tied to the mission, that is the ultimate users, whether they are intelligence users, military users, or whomever.

Big organizational changes come with long-term impacts. I reorganized the NRO almost totally in 1992. It was the right thing to do, but it took 10 years for the NRO to fully work through that. The current situation I would start by asking the Secretary of Defense to review what do all the people who interact with space do and is there value added?

I would measure the response by constantly examining what happens to the program manager, the person actually getting something done? When the program manager starts the journey, what happens along the way? If the program manager's life is getting better, we are on the road to success.

Thank you, and I look forward to your questions.

[The prepared statement of Mr. Faga can be found in the Appendix on page 58.]

Mr. ROGERS. I thank all the witnesses for those outstanding opening statements.

Now I will recognize myself for the first questions. And I want to start by trying to help us understand the challenges that we face. And I would tell all the witnesses, I am going to ask for a yes or no answer, but don't worry. In just a minute on the second part of this question you will get to expand. So don't feel like I am boxing you in.

I would ask each one of you, do you believe that we are currently adequately postured to address the serious challenges faced in space?

Dr. Hamre.

Dr. HAMRE. No.

Mr. ELLIS. No, I do not, sir.

Mr. FAGA. No.

Mr. ROGERS. Great. Let me ask this. Why do you believe that, Dr. Hamre, and just be succinct and try to abbreviate your—in a nutshell what you think is the reason why we are not adequately prepared?

Dr. HAMRE. I do not think that we have exercised the appropriate strategic leadership probably for 15 years on space. This problem has been growing. It is far more dangerous than we realize. We have not challenged the combatant commanders to understand their vulnerabilities.

We have not done a stress test to really know what would happen to us. We have been too preoccupied with getting a broad space policy right without operationalizing it and turning it into real doctrine.

Mr. ROGERS. Okay.

Admiral Ellis, why not?

Admiral ELLIS. I would echo Dr. Hamre's comments. We have been surprised. We assumed space would always be the sanctuary it was 15 or 20 years ago. The technology and the threat has outpaced our creation of policy and strategy appropriate to the need. Most importantly, we lack significant capabilities.

We are playing catch-up in a very real sense, but it is not just about hardware and technology. A lot of it is about policies that deal, as I said earlier in my opening remarks, at the strategic level. What is it we stand for? What is it we will accept? What are the concepts of deterrence that are appropriate for this new domain? That conversation, while under way now, is beginning and you can look back, as the committee has, at virtually two decades of studies that have highlighted this both on the procurement side and on the operational and policy side.

So I think we got surprised, quite frankly, and a number of people along the way predicted that possibility even and now we find ourselves playing catch-up in a very real sense. A lot is under way. The awareness is certainly there.

You hear it and see it in a lot of the products and writings and things that are being produced, particularly within the Air Force. But unfortunately I don't think we are moving at a pace that is going to close the gap that needs to be closed very, very quickly.

Mr. ROGERS. Mr. Faga, why are we not prepared?

Mr. FAGA. I would start off by saying we say quite a bit about this in our NRC study, which is available free online to anybody. We don't fully know how to respond.

The experience that General Hyten had of realizing the combatant commanders can't yet tell him what capability they need, how will their war plans change, and what backups will they use? What non-space assets could be pursued? We don't have all of that. We don't have all that worked out.

As Admiral Ellis testified, there are things we can do. Arrangements with allies, codes of conduct, deterrence measures, things we can do at the strategic level that will help the situation.

This is a problem really only fully recognized, in my view, in 2014. I will have to say, as Admiral Ellis said, lots going on in the Pentagon, but it certainly hasn't come together to an adequate answer to the question you asked.

Mr. ROGERS. Well, I think that the degree of exposure has heightened in the last couple of years and probably since 2014, but Admiral Ellis is right. This has been recognized for nearly two decades as a problem area and studied to death for 2 years, which leads me to my next question.

Do you think this is a problem the DOD can correct itself or will it need to be compelled by statute to do something in particular to remedy the situation? And I will leave that to anybody who wants to answer.

Mr. Faga.

Mr. FAGA. So in my mid-career, I spent time as a staff member on the House Intelligence Committee staff. And one of the things I watched and learned is the first thing you want to do is lay out for the Department what the problem is and ask them to come up with a solution so that they do that inside the construct in which they live. It probably won't be adequate.

And secondly, they will need legislation from you for powers they don't currently have. But I think it starts with, let them tell you what they need to do.

Admiral ELLIS. Mr. Chairman, as we talked in your office, I am very reluctant personally when I am outside an organization to offer prescriptive comments on exactly how they need to reorganize.

It goes back to my days as a young test pilot when I would find a deficiency in a new aircraft and I was cautioned, never tell the contractor or the designer what to do to fix it, because if he does what you told him to do and it doesn't fix it or it has unintended consequences, you are liable and the program is no further along. The better approach is to tell him this problem needs to be fixed and let him use his creativity and insight to do that. Now, he needs to be held accountable for that corrective action there is no doubt. So I would only suggest that DOD, with the right level of understanding, which I believe that they have now on the seriousness of this, ought to be asked and expected to identify whether the changes that they put in place have delivered on the promise that they expected, whether the timelines are reduced, whether effi- ciencies are being realized, whether this collaborative process is working.

My personal view, and I think I am aligned with Dr. Hamre in this regard, is we need to put somebody in charge and give them the authorities and the accountability for outcomes, not aspirations.

But I would encourage them to be given the opportunity to shape an organizational structure that best suits their needs. It is kind of like where you put the sidewalks on a college campus. In organizational structures you put the sidewalks where the paths are worn in the grass. And so within the organization, who needs to talk to each other, who needs to communicate in order to get the job done ought to be the way they begin to pursue organizational realignment.

Mr. ROGERS. Thank you.

Dr. Hamre.

Dr. HAMRE. You know, it is the Congress that establishes national goals and gives direction to the executive branch to undertake them. I would think it is best for the Congress not to tell the executive branch how to accomplish those goals, but we have watched 20 years where this has not come together.

And I ask myself why has it not come together? And I think it is because internally we have been fractured. And it has been hard to sustain a focus in the Department, common across the board. So I, I do think you are going to have to put pressure to get this done right and you have an opportunity with a change of administration coming.

And I think you should think about concrete things that need to be done in a 3-year window, because that is roughly the window of a Secretary, and an 8-year window, roughly the time horizon an administration is in office and accountable, and then the past 8 years.

And I think each of the tasks we need in each of those categories will be equally urgent, but I think we need to disaggregate the nature of this problem. Because right now we are too diffuse——

Mr. ROGERS. Right.

Dr. HAMRE [continuing]. And we are not coming up with answers to these problems.

Mr. ROGERS. Well, thank you. Before I yield to the ranking member, I wanted to point out just to give you some, everybody in the room some idea about how difficult this problem is. The GAO stated space acquisition management and oversight is fragmented across 60 stakeholders.

So I asked the GAO to put together an organizational chart just so we could get a good mind's eye view of what it is like. They said it was too complicated to put a chart together. So what they gave me was this list of—I don't know what it is a list of, just complexities.

So I had my staff try to put together an organizational chart, and this is it. Nobody has got line authority to make decisions, and this org chart has to be simplified.

[The chart referred to can be found in the Appendix on page 69.]

Mr. ROGERS. So with that, no pressure, ranking member, you tell us how we are going to simplify it.

Mr. COOPER. Thank you, Mr. Chairman. I share your commitment to enhance our space capabilities. I do think it is important to point out, though, that we have much to be proud of, what we have today. I think none of the witnesses would want to trade our capability with that of any other nation. So I think, really, more the question is preserving our margin of excellence over any possible rival.

I appreciate your testimony and the accumulated wisdom that you all have. There are many ways to fix a problem. I hope that the next Congress will be able to tackle this issue based on the foundation that the chairman is laying.

Dr. Hamre, in your testimony, you talked about some pockets of excellence that are out there, things that even by our desire to enhance our program are still performing at near peak levels, and I think you mentioned NRO.

Mr. Faga mentioned program managers as generally excellent in what they do. Would you share his enthusiasm for that level of what Air Force colonel that is out there making projects happen? Dr. HAMRE. Well, the NRO has had a demonstrated history of really quite high performance. You know, in general, I think our acquisition system has declined over the last 30 years. I hate to say it.

I think it is in large measure because we have elevated the gunsmithing of buying things above the marksmanship questions of what we are trying to do. And I, you know, I just—I hate to say this, but we need to go back and revisit the Packard Commission and the way we created the institutions recommended in the Packard Commission.

We have created a giant compliance organization in the building. It used to be that a brilliant colonel with a couple of briefings could be in front of the Secretary of Defense within weeks. You know, now it takes a couple of, it takes months, maybe even a year for a good idea to get in front of the Secretary. And the steps along the way are just unbelievable. So broadly, the acquisition system, in my view, is failing us.

Mr. COOPER. That is, indeed, a big task, but Chairman Thornberry is working to try to improve that. One of you gentlemen pointed out to us before the hearing that there were many fewer challenges, contractor contests of bids, you know, 10, 20, 30 years ago, but now it is almost a routine matter.

So when you mentioned compliance, I think you are really talking about making something challenge-proof once the contract is awarded, right? This is kind of gold-plating the procurement process so that it is incredibly slow, and by the time the technology is fielded, it is largely out of date.

Another important aspect of the overall testimony was Admiral Ellis' focus on the global commons and comparing it with the way the seas were viewed, you know, a long time ago. Establishing some sort of international framework for this or even establishing our own warfighting rules is going to be a challenge.

And I look forward to receiving your guidance on that, because these are indeed complex matters and probably no one has thought through all the implications of what needs to be done.

I found particularly interesting Mr. Faga's trust in the program managers and his management philosophy that if you empower them and get all the distractions out of the way, they will be able to do a better job.

Mr. Faga, if you could describe for us briefly the career path of these program managers? We talked about this briefly before the hearing and about when they exit the Air Force or the service and then what they move on to?

Mr. FAGA. I did describe a career path, unfortunately one seldom followed today, but it typically starts as as a junior officer or civilian at a subsystem project level, then moves up to project manager for a subsystem. It usually involves an operational tour of some kind.

At some point a director of engineering in the SPO [system program office], commander of a ground site, deputy program manager, program manager, and that typically took about 20 years. And as I said to you, nobody ever contested those colonels.

When I was at the NRO, I called them the great colonels. And when I talk to some of them today, 20-some years later, I still say the great colonels. But we are not doing that kind of development nearly as much today, whether in the NRO or in the Air Force.

It is one of the reasons I pushed hard a few years ago, successfully ultimately, to get a permanent engineering cadre in the NRO, which it did not have and which it is now building. My view being this is very complicated stuff and people need to spend 20 or 30 years doing it, not an occasional tour.

Mr. COOPER. You pointed out something to me I found very interesting, that these colonels actually shunned promotion.

Mr. FAGA. Again, we are talking a time in the past, but I would speak to lieutenant colonels and say, look, you have got to get out of the NRO. I will help you get a great assignment in a regular— you can't get promoted maybe even to colonel, certainly not to general.

Every single one of them said, "I don't care. I believe in this work. I like the organization. I will retire as a lieutenant colonel or a colonel. I will go into the industry. Please don't worry about me anymore."

Mr. COOPER. So it sounds like part of it was the passion for their project, but part of it was an alternative career path that was as attractive for them or more attractive than becoming a general.

Mr. FAGA. Frankly, the most successful post-military careers are colonels who are in their late forties or early fifties, plenty of runway. Many of them became vice presidents in the business, and they knew that. They knew that. But frankly to them it wasn't the rank or the money. It was, "I can stay in the business. I can keep doing this."

Mr. COOPER. So perhaps we on the committee need to understand that real world relationship and take that into account. One thing that I have worried about for a long time is the punch-your-ticket mentality where people do an assignment for 2 or 3 years, but by the time they get good at it they get promoted out of there and you lose that expertise that you are training into them all the time.

But another facet seems to be that some of these extraordinary performers are being taken by private industry. And they lead very productive commercial lives then but we lose their military expertise. So figuring out that relationship is something that we are going to have to be able to do, as is having fewer layers of management over these people so that there is less red tape to cut through. I thank you, Mr. Chairman. Perhaps we will have time for another round of questioning.

Mr. ROGERS. We will. I thank the gentleman.

The Chair now recognizes gentleman from Arizona, Mr. Franks, for 5 minutes.

Mr. FRANKS. Well, thank you, Mr. Chairman, and thank all of you for being here. It is always encouraging to me to have people like you thinking and doing the things necessary to help protect our children. I have got 8-year-old twins and I really like them, and I really appreciate you guys for watching out for them.

Admiral Ellis, I was particularly impressed with your testimony and I wanted to ask you, what is your understanding of the arrangements there in place between the DOD and the Intelligence Community as it relates to the various commercial companies regarding the U.S. Government's ability to task and use those commercial satellites that we have in space in times of crisis or wartime?

Admiral ELLIS. Well, thank you, Mr. Franks. There are a couple of dimensions or a couple of levels to that. First off, as we have noted earlier, there is a nascent effort to bring on the operational side the private sector, the civilians into the JICSpOC [Joint Interagency Combined Space Operations Center], and as you are well aware and bring a presence there.

The authorities do not yet exist, as I understand it, for DOD to exercise actual control over those resources and the like. But at least they are communicating to the extent that classification levels permit, which is, again, an issue that we have to deal with sometimes.

The space situational awareness, the information that we have we can't share with the commercial colleagues. So on the operational side there is movement and some low levels of progress.

On the procurement side, as Mr. Faga has already indicated, I think DOD is recognizing that the improvements and enhance-ments in the private sector capabilities that are resident on orbit are absolutely staggering, and in many cases offer a more ubiq- uitous, if you will, presence and ability to draw unnoticed perhaps that would not necessarily be resident in a DOD dedicated system. And you have to assume that our adversaries know exactly what the orbital parameters are and when the television camera is over- head and the like. And the more of those things on which we can draw, I think, the better.

But I don't, and my impression is, I don't have, you know, up- to-date information as of today, but the contracting vehicles that Marty referred to earlier, the ability to buy this access on a regular basis on the spot market, to make long-term commitments that would allow the private sector to grow those capabilities even more given a level of certainty in terms of the DOD being a reliable cus- tomer is not yet where it would need to be to close the business model, if you make the case.

And don't misunderstand me. These folks are patriots, too. Not every patriot wears uniforms. They are trying to do what they can to support the national security needs of the Nation and have for many, many years.

But they are frustrated by their inability to deal over the long term. They are having to make business decisions, talk to share-holders and make financial commitments and yet they don't have certainty as to the long-term character of DOD's relationship.

And those things need to be addressed and can be to create the kind of system we want, a national security space enterprise that, as I said in my testimony, that essentially redefines what national security space looks like. It isn't just the NRO. It isn't just the DOD.

It is the commercial sector, and not just the communications, as important as that is, but now the imagery and the like that can come from those resources. And that has the potential to be a much more reliable and resilient system. And so we need to move and improve in that situation.

Mr. FRANKS. Well, I might, Dr. Hamre, let me, if I could, expand the question a little bit and then pass it over to you. Given what I am hearing from Admiral Ellis, that we don't have all of those things figured out just yet as far as what we can use and cannot use, what are the most time-sensitive reforms we have to imple-ment in order to be prepared for a conflict that either begins or spreads into space? And what is your understanding of our ability to use some of those private resources?

Dr. HAMRE. Well, sir, what I wanted to bring to the committee's attention, we do this right now in aviation. We have something called the Civil Reserve Air Fleet.

We pay commercial airlines money to put features into commer-cial aircraft so that they are useful for us for military purposes. We give them a subsidy every year for carrying around that dead weight because it is important to us.

When they are mobilized, we indemnify those aircraft. We use them in wartime. We have a model that we could use for space, probably have to be adapted in some ways, but we have a model. And it exists. It is legal. It has been proven out in our system.

So this is something we can do. And I really would think it would be an important contribution for your committee to develop the architecture for that.

Mr. FRANKS. Thank you, Mr. Chairman.

Mr. ROGERS. Thank the gentleman.

The Chair now recognizes the gentleman from California, Mr. Aguilar, for 5 minutes.

Mr. AGUILAR. Thank you, Mr. Chairman. Admiral Ellis, in your testimony you pointed to one of GAO's proposals, the creation of a defense space agency as the one to clearly define responsibilities, leadership, and authorities for the oversight of military space.

In your opinion and if some of the other witnesses could also comment, what are some of the risks you foresee if the defense space agency were to be created?

Admiral ELLIS. I am sorry. For clarification, sir, you want the risks, the downsides of that?

Mr. AGUILAR. Correct. Correct.

Admiral ELLIS. Well, as you may recall, in a proposal that I endorsed for that, it was primarily focused on the procurement and not on the operational side. But I think some would view it as a negative that it didn't include all national security space.

In other words, the way I see it, because of the capabilities and the efficiencies and the better performance we have seen in the NRO, I did not believe and do not believe that homogenizing that by bringing it and all its capabilities under the Department of Defense is a thing to do. So it would not in that sense oversee all of the national security space.

It would require some legislative relief. That is not necessarily a problem, but it could be and that is certainly your area of expertise and not mine. And it does have, as do all changes that are proposed or addressed by the GAO other than the do-nothing option, has the potential for some level of disruption.

But, you know, we have given this opportunity for change two decades now. And we have seen some here in the last couple of years, particularly within the Air Force, certainly a focus from the Office of the Secretary of Defense on this.

The question is is this making a difference? Is this enough? Is this kind of an incremental approach that isn't yet delivering on the potential and the needs to improve the process?

So again, I am not a big favor of dramatic increases in bureaucracy. I am not a big fan of precipitous and unthoughtful action, but we have got to do something different than we have been doing to get a different outcome.

And so that is the reason that I believe that raising this to the Under Secretary of Defense level, the accountability for space, and as I said in my opening remarks, being accountable for outcomes and not aspirations is hugely important. But with that have to come the authorities and the responsibilities that enable that be happening, to happen, so——

Mr. AGUILAR. Others on risks?

Dr. HAMRE. I would say I think the downside in my view of this is that we will look at this as a military hardware-only solution.

You create an organization that is designed to build military hardware, that is all they are going to do.

And I think the architecture of survival and resilience going forward is going to be far more dependent on commercial platforms and diversification of our capacities than it is about buying military stuff. We are really good at building reconnaissance satellites—really good. But we can only afford to buy one or two of them.

You know, we need to find a totally different way where we are putting much more of our focus on what the private sector can give us and how we would use that. And we have put a provocative thought in front of you but, you know, I think the average number of airmen it takes to maintain a satellite's constellation is like 700. But the average number of people you would find in a commercial satellite operation running a satellite network is 10, okay? And there is just a different world here, and we have got to start thinking about how do we tap into the private sector and the capabilities that they can give us that we could use?

And I think the only reason—I am not arguing with Jim's recommendation, Admiral Ellis' recommendation, but it would again lock us into thinking we have to have military answers to this problem. I would like us to have commercial things.

Mr. AGUILAR. Sure.

Mr. Faga.

Mr. FAGA. Many advantages which the NRO enjoys, almost all of them are externally granted, so this isn't something that came from within. There is an organization in DOD that is similar, Missile Defense Agency [MDA].

In fact, it is fascinating. I was amazed, in fact, in a study not too long ago, to look at the charter and the authorities of the director of MDA, a charter written around 2002 or so. It reads like the 1961 charter of the NRO. It is absolutely amazing. And frankly, dealing with a very, very difficult problem, I think they have worked wonders.

So we do have examples inside of DOD that I think are instructive.

Mr. AGUILAR. Thank you. I yield back, Mr. Chairman.

Mr. ROGERS. I thank the gentleman.

The Chair now recognizes the gentleman from Colorado, Mr. Lamborn, for 5 minutes.

Mr. LAMBORN. Thank you, Mr. Chairman, for having this important hearing. And I want to thank each of the panelists for your presentation. In 10 years this is one of the best presentations I have ever been witness to, so thank you.

You have all referred to snippets of what the problem is and I want to ask each of you to define as concisely as possible what it is we need to solve. I have heard you quote Admiral Rickover "If everyone has responsibility no one has responsibility." General Hyten was quoted to the effect that resilience has only now recently become a priority.

It takes too long to bring assets online and there are too many layers of reporting and review. But what is it that we need to solve? Could you each state that for the help of myself and the rest of the committee?

Admiral ELLIS. Well, sir, and it can sound overly simplistic, and I don't mean it this way. You have touched on a number of the dimensions. And this is a multifaceted problem. There isn't just one single element.

But in the end, it always comes down to leadership. It always comes down to a commitment on the part of those that are responsible for this that they believe passionately and that they have the authorities they need to do it. They have the accountability and that they are comfortable with, and they go out and get it done. Now, that sounds simplistic, and I don't mean it that way. There is a lot of detail underneath all of that. Organizational? Yes. Technical? Certainly. Resiliency I talked about in my statement.

All those things are the kinds of things that the leader needs to bring into focus. But it needs to be done, and it can't just be talked about. It just can't be reviewed. We don't need another study and the like.

We know, I think in our hearts, what needs to be accomplished. We just need to have the courage to go out and do it.

Dr. HAMRE. Sir, I would say we are coming up on a new administration. If I was in your position, what I would demand is that the Secretary and the Chairman of the Joint Chiefs do a stress test of all of our war plans on what happens with plausible space denial action by opponents.

We will know where we are if you do a real stress——

Mr. LAMBORN. Which I think is what JICSpOC is supposed to help resolve?

Dr. HAMRE. Well, the Secretary needs to do this and the Chairman needs to do this.

Mr. LAMBORN. Okay.

Dr. HAMRE. This has to be at the very top in my personal view.

Mr. LAMBORN. Okay.

Dr. HAMRE. And then the second thing that needs to be done immediately is a cyber evaluation. I personally believe the easiest way for the opponents to get in is through cyber. And I personally believe they are probably already there. We cannot afford to find that out in the start of a war. We need to figure out where we are for reliability now.

And then the longer term is how are we going to get greater diversity and use of private sector assets? We buy it, we pay for it, you know, we rent it, whatever, so we are not entirely dependent on these great big expensive, small number of platforms that are easy to attack.

Mr. LAMBORN. Mr. Faga.

Mr. FAGA. So who is in charge of military air? Who is the one person in charge of military air? All four services do it. There is no one person in charge. And the reason for that is it is very complex. All the services are engaged, OSD [Office of the Secretary of Defense] engaged. It is a fundamental capability.

I don't mean that the stewardship of it isn't good. I think it is because it is well-developed. It is well-established. This is all new for the space community. That is why my view is just looking for the right person to attach all of those spaghetti lines to is not the answer.

Everybody has got work to do here. People want to make the acquisition process faster. I certainly do. In fact, in my early years in the NRO as an engineer, our standard planning number for a new system was 42 months to delivery, and we routinely met it. But there are policy issues. There is the education of the combat- ant commands who all say they need it but don't fully understand its significance.

There are jobs for everybody to do and it takes leadership, just as it takes leadership in the services to run their air assets, which in the Navy is only one of several major assets.

I would want to look at the multifaceted problem that we have here more than look for, who was that person that I can put in charge of everything?

Mr. LAMBORN. Thank you all.

I yield back, Mr. Chairman.

Mr. ROGERS. I thank the gentleman.

The Chair now recognizes the gentleman from Oklahoma, Mr. Bridenstine, for 5 minutes.

Mr. BRIDENSTINE. Well, I appreciate that, Mr. Chairman. It is an honor to be here with you gentlemen. The folks that work in our space industry today stand on the shoulders of giants, and you are those giants. And it is great to have you before this committee.

I would like to start by saying I have read a number of the, maybe not recommendations, but the different options that have been presented by the three of you.

One that I think is of particular interest is the idea of the reestablishment of a U.S. Space Command, not just Air Force Space Command, but a U.S. Space Command.

In other words, a functional combatant command similar, you mentioned, Dr. Hamre, similar to what we see with SOCOM, where in effect you have a functional combatant command, but it also has some responsibility to do the man, train, and equip mission. Is that kind of what you were thinking when you said that?

Dr. HAMRE. Yes, sir. I think, as I mentioned, there are three circles of leadership which we have to have in the Department. You have to have the organizational title 10. You are bringing together the resources, buying things, training people, et cetera.

You have to have——

Mr. BRIDENSTINE. But that would normally fall under one of the four services, the service——

Dr. HAMRE. Yes, sir, although we do have things like the Missile Defense Agency, which stands outside.

Mr. BRIDENSTINE. Okay.

Dr. HAMRE. SOCOM has unique acquisition authorities we gave it when we created SOCOM. So you could create special acquisition authorities and give it to the Space Command. I think they would be wise to use the fairly considerable infrastructure that already exists but have leadership capacities at the Space Command.

Then you have to have operational responsibility. That is what they do every day at Space Command, but it needs to be for everybody. We need to make this a joint thing. And then you have to have strategic leadership, and that is where you need to have, as Admiral Ellis said, you need to have a focus in the Pentagon, somebody in the Pentagon.

SOCOM has the Assistant Secretary for Special Operations. He has a counterpart in the Pentagon. We have to have a leadership counterpart in the Pentagon. I think that is what you are hearing from this group.

Mr. BRIDENSTINE. Okay. And the reason that intrigues me is because one of the questions that the chairman asked was, what does it require from Congress?

And creating a combatant command, my understanding is the Secretary of Defense has the authority to disestablish a combatant command or establish a combatant command, which means it really wouldn't require anything from us other than the strategic guidance that Congress wants to see a unified command responsible for this kind of capability, which I believe is critically important.

One of the things that concerns me is we have to make sure that we are keeping separate the idea of a combatant command from the man, train, and equip mission. I understand there is overlap. There has to be overlap.

One of the other things that intrigued me about what you wrote was that—and I think, Admiral Ellis, you mentioned a similar thing, creating a service within the Air Force much like maybe the Army Air Service was to the Army, much like the Marine Corps is today to the Navy, where you have got different officer progressions, you have got different budgets, but you report to the same, ultimately the same service secretary.

It doesn't seem like having a space combatant command would necessarily be separate from having a space service within the Air Force that might have a different organizational structure.

Not going as far as to be disruptive in creating a separate service, but within the Air Force having a service that is dedicated specifically to that, is that, the two are not mutually exclusive. Is that correct? That is really my question.

Dr. HAMRE. Well, I should rely on Admiral Ellis, because he is the military officer here. I think that you need his judgment on this question more than mine.

Mr. BRIDENSTINE. Yes.

Admiral ELLIS. Well, as some of you may be aware, I was in command of the United States Strategic Command when U.S. Space Command was merged with it. And it was done not because space was unimportant, but because space was so important that it needed to be brought in even closer alignment with the warfighter.

And, as you may recall, we completed the first nuclear posture review and determined that we are redefining the term "strategic." Strategic used to be and used to mean nuclear.

Mr. BRIDENSTINE. Right.

Admiral ELLIS. And then it was expanded to include all capabilities with strategic impact.

Mr. BRIDENSTINE. Right.

Admiral ELLIS. And they included everything, I mean, global strike, missile defense, that hated acronym C4ISR [command, control, communications, computers, intelligence, surveillance, and reconnaissance] and all of those things, all of which relied so heavily on space assets. The intent was to bring those more closely in alignment and use that reduction to improve and enhance the creation and oversight of those capabilities.

But to your point, sir, if you were to create a new strategic command or a space command, you would be using the same elements that already exist, and——

Mr. BRIDENSTINE. Okay.

Admiral ELLIS [continuing]. And you would create a headquarters, because everything is operated through component structures as you are well aware from——

Mr. BRIDENSTINE. Sure.

Admiral ELLIS [continuing]. From your military background. But, it would also draw from the pool of space experts that exist within the services and departments for its manning and staffing.

So I would argue that, again, I am not necessarily a big fan of an organizational change just to do that, because I really don't think that the operational piece is as much the issue.

The issue, as we focused on a lot here, is procurement——

Mr. BRIDENSTINE. Right.

Admiral ELLIS [continuing]. Of the tools and the systems that our space warfighters need, and quite frankly, that is not the role of a combatant command. They can provide requirements, but they don't buy or oversee those kinds of processes. That is an organize, train, and equip function.

Mr. BRIDENSTINE. I am out of time, but I want to make this one last—in 2001, there was a report that came out from a commission on organization and management of national security space chaired by Donald Rumsfeld before he was Secretary of Defense.

And that commission explicitly stated what you said, which is within the Air Force, you have got the people that generate the requirements. Those are the operators. And then you have got the people who do the purchasing. And those are not the same people. And that creates a disconnect.

And in the commission report, it actually specified the NRO as the agency that actually does it right, where the operators are directly involved in the acquisition. And because of that, when there is an anomaly in a space system, the operators know the difference between an anomaly and an attack. And that is a very important thing.

So I think when we think about acquisitions as it comes to space, we need to think about it differently than when we buy a tank or something else.

So with that, Mr. Chairman, I will yield back.

Mr. ROGERS. I thank the gentleman.

I recognize myself for the next series of questions. Mr. Bridenstine just made the observation about the NRO, which we have talked about. They do it right. I mean they do it much better. And when you look at the director of the NRO, they have direct report to the Secretary of Defense—or not the Secretary of Defense, the Under Secretary for Intelligence and then the DNI. And then the rest of military space is this. I mean, it just seems like we have got to find something comparable if we are going to get the sort of efficacy that we see at the NRO.

One of the options that the GAO report offered was the PDSA, the Principal DOD Space Advisor. And some of the departments say that, you know, taking the Secretary of the Air Force and changing the title from executive agent to PDSA is the solution, and we are in the first year of that.

My problem with that is the A, advisor. If the Secretary of the Air Force is an advisor, who is in charge? So tell me what I am missing? It seems to me that we have changed the title, and we have moved the deck chairs around on the ship, but we haven't changed the direction of the ship. Somebody tell me why I am wrong.

Mr. Faga.

Dr. HAMRE. Sir, I don't think you are wrong. I mean, it is—again, I don't personally believe the Secretary can alienate his responsibility for bringing focus to what we are doing as a department. And it is very hard to assign that to a subordinate entity and have everybody else take that person seriously.

Mr. ROGERS. Perfect question, does the Secretary of the Air Force him- or herself have time to do this? Are they just going to delegate it to somebody?

Dr. HAMRE. You know, 30 years ago when I think it worked well, it was actually the Under Secretary of the Air Force whose job it was to run space. But that was because it was the Secretary's priority, and the Secretary backed that individual up, and everybody in the building knew that was the Secretary's person.

I just don't hear that when I talk to people in the Department right now that there is a clarity of who is responsible and who is actually running things for space.

Mr. ROGERS. Should the Secretary of the Air Force be in charge of all DOD space?

Dr. HAMRE. Well, you have to empower the secretary to have the Secretary's authority. I mean the only way that works is when the Secretary of Defense says, that person will decide for me, and I haven't heard that.

Mr. ROGERS. So are you saying it should be an OSD joint command?

Dr. HAMRE. No, sir.

Mr. ROGERS. Or joint responsibility, rather?

Dr. HAMRE. Again, my personal view is things really function— you know, the Department has a balance between line organizations and staff organizations. Line organizations are those that really run things, the service chiefs. They run these military departments. We have some defense agencies that are line organizations.

Everything in OSD, and to include the Secretary of the Air Force is line responsible, but only for things in the Air Force.

Mr. ROGERS. Right.

Dr. HAMRE. Nobody in the Navy is going to think that they are going to take an order from the Secretary of the Air Force.

Mr. ROGERS. So by virtue of what you are just saying, it should be an OSD responsibility?

Dr. HAMRE. Sir, I think it needs to be a combination of OSD oversight and military line responsibility and how you get that— you can do it through a defense agency. You can do it through a unified command. But you need to have somebody who is going to work every day, that is their job. They are not simply advising the Secretary in what they think that person should do.

Mr. ROGERS. Mr. Faga.

Mr. FAGA. I want to talk about your point about advisor by pointing out the secretary in her Air Force Secretary role is doing 90 percent of military space in terms of acquisition. Ninety percent of it is in the Air Force.

The Navy program is tiny and that is about it. Army program is mostly support equipment. So she has already got most of it. Now, the significance of being the principal advisor means she can go direct to the SECDEF [Secretary of Defense]. In the big bureaucracy of the Pentagon and as senior as she is, that is a big deal.

It is a privilege I enjoyed when I was the director of the NRO. And once in a while, someone somewhere else in the bureaucracy would decide to take me on. We went to the Secretary. They lost. That was that.

I think she has the same opportunities, so I am not as ready to give up on it as others may be. We will see. We will see.

It is also the case that Secretary James is pretty engaged and energetic. I think she is having some success. Because in examining all of these questions, I come back to who is in charge of military air or many other functions that exist within the Department?

So I think she is pretty well-situated. She is the third ranking official in the Department, pretty well-situated.

Mr. ROGERS. Yes, I would say, first of all, this has got nothing to do with Secretary James particularly. It has more to do with the position. Now, she is an extraordinarily competent lady.

This is about the Secretary of the Air Force being charged with this advisor role when I don't see it being given the decision-making authority and control of the money to implement decisions and then the responsibility for success.

And also, I frankly don't see this as being the Air Force's primary mission. I think it has been my experience in the last few years that it seems that space is always going to take a back seat in the Air Force, and that bothers me. That may be an erroneous observation on my part, but it is one that concerns me.

Yes, sir, Dr. Hamre.

Dr. HAMRE. Mr. Chairman—and I don't want to pick a fight with my two colleagues, who are far more expert on this than I am, but, you know, we have war plans that depend on space today, and they will fail if space is attacked.

Mr. ROGERS. Right.

Dr. HAMRE. Well, I don't see the Secretary of the Air Force solving that problem. I mean, this has got to be the Chairman of the Joint Chiefs that is doing a stress test of all of his war plans with his commanders. The Chairman of the Joint Chiefs does not report to the Secretary of the Air Force.

Mr. ROGERS. That is the whole reason why this has taken such a priority for this committee. If we are going to fight a war successfully, we have to have space control, and the attributes that it brings. And if, those are vulnerable now. It is just the facts. So this has to be addressed.

All right, I will stop there and turn over to the ranking member for his additional questions.

Mr. COOPER. Thank you, Mr. Chairman. This has been a very productive discussion. I was wondering if we need to have a similar hearing, though, on establishing some sort of enhanced cyber command?

Dr. Hamre mentioned that perhaps our greatest vulnerability with satellites is through cyber. But each of these domains seem to be requiring greater attention and more flexibility from the bureaucracy so that we can live up to our full potential. So would you gentleman each suggest that we have a similar discussion regarding cyber the way we are doing space today?

Admiral ELLIS. Yeah, I certainly think that dialogue is essential, sir. I think there are some real parallels here. We have challenges in the cyber domain with attribution, knowing who actually did the act that we now discover is being, you know, performed against us. Same thing can be true in space. Is it debris when your satellite fails or was it a nefarious act on the part of another actor? And you know, there are some parallels, and I think that kind of over- sight and understanding, but it also highlights a lot of the same complexities in all of this.

If you create a standalone cyber command, what is the impact of that drawing expertise from the services that may be in short supply to stand up that command? And what are the implications of moving cyber both offense and defense into the warfighting domain of the combatant commanders, which was the intent?

I mean it is as Dr. Hamre said, and as I said in my prepared testimony, every organizational alignment is sub-optimized for something. You just have to decide what your priorities are.

Is it what is most important or is what you do the most? The two are not necessarily the same. And so how you structure that, there are going to be some pluses and minuses in every structure. And I think you are hearing that from my colleagues here, and all of them with good inputo.

Mr. COOPER. There is general agreement on that?

Mr. FAGA. Yeah.

Admiral ELLIS. Yeah.

Mr. COOPER. To sell a new space command or some sort of an enhanced space capability to the American people and perhaps to our own colleagues, it is going to be very important that they understand the significance of satellites.

And I noted in Mr. Faga's testimony he quoted General Formica as saying that "Every company commander depends on space and they all take it for granted." You know?

[Laughter.]

You know, if every captain is dependent that means everybody who wears a uniform is dependent on it. And I know in the private sector I know some people who can't play golf without relying on a satellite.

[Laughter.]

But some people can't play anyway, but——

[Laughter.]

And it is a hard sport. But it almost makes me think of having a satellite-free day to enhance the awareness of the importance of satellites except for the fact that satellites are already so critical that that would devastate the economy in probably every nation in the world if we were to try to go without the timing functions and other functions that are hidden deep in the background of every ATM or every machine we depend on.

So we are already beyond the point at which we could deprive ourselves voluntarily of this capability, but that is exactly probably what the enemy is thinking about doing to us in the event of an attack to bind us before we even knew we were attacked and then to probably disguise that as a debris strike and have us in a quandary for a while before we knew who to blame.

Mr. Faga.

Mr. FAGA. Sir, the military plays this as a war game in what they call Schriever Games. I would strongly recommend that you get their classified briefing on some of the their recent games on exactly the point you have just raised, Mr. Cooper.

You would find it revealing.

Mr. COOPER. Finally let me end with the point that if we want to live up to our full military potential and do the right thing then, A, we would fully fund our troops, which we haven't been doing for about 15 years now, using devices like OCO [overseas contingency operations] funding and things like that in which we basically are asking for the Chinese and other international creditors to help pay our bills.

B, we would clear up some of these bureaucratic oversight lines ourselves. I think the Department of Homeland Security reports to some 60 congressional committees or subcommittees; the satellite area is probably almost as confusing. And my colleague Mr. Bridenstine's excellent point having the operator and the acquirer be more the same people then they know what is going on.

Well, we have, of course have this ancient divide between authorizing committees here and appropriators and only the appropriators really matter.

[Laughter.]

Yeah, that is right. So we have a lot of housecleaning to do here on this side of the dais. But I thank you, gentlemen, for your excellent testimony. It has been very thought-provoking.

Mr. ROGERS. I thank the gentleman.

The Chair now recognizes the gentleman from Colorado, Mr. Lamborn, for a second 5 minutes.

Mr. LAMBORN. Thank you. I would like to drill down with each of you on the slow acquisition process. That is one of the major facets of the problem we are trying to deal with. And I would like to mention that I recently met with a commercial SATCOM provider who can order a new satellite from Lockheed Martin and have it built and launched within 24 months.

And yet Lockheed also provides to DOD but not on a 24-month schedule, and so I don't think it is Lockheed. What is it, why do we have such slow acquisition schedules?

Mr. Faga.

Mr. FAGA. Because it takes a very long time to decide what it is we are going to build, even if the decision after a couple of years of effort is we are going to build exactly what we have already got. When a SATCOM operator goes to Lockheed, first of all they are saying we want to use the standard bus.

You know, I want array of transponders that looks roughly like this. There isn't very much design work. There is no new engineering. It is really just building something pretty close to what you sold me last time and due in 24 months.

It is also interesting their approach to how to maintain their constellation. Even at NRO we used to go through these great design life studies and calculations and recalculations.

What SATCOM operators tend to say is I have got a 50-some satellite constellation. I have got three satellites on orbit that are spares, and I have got two or three of them on the ground ready for launch.

Getting to launch can be really slow. It can take months. I might mention in that regard that I once had the opportunity to visit the Arianespace launch facility in Kourou in French Guiana. And their system was all designed from the ground up pretty much in the 1980s.

The whole system is integrated. They can fly different sizes of their satellites off the same pad. Platform heights are the same. Electrical plug-ins are the same all the way up and down.

With that kind of modern infrastructure, they can launch very quickly. We don't have that capacity in the United States.

Mr. LAMBORN. Admiral Ellis.

Admiral ELLIS. Yes, sir. It is a great question, and in fairness there are differences that we levy on national security assets. Now, you can ask a fair question and I think you have. How much of that should be done in the exquisite designs that we custom-tailor, as the Brits would say bespoke creation for national security purposes.

Sometimes they are legitimate requirements. EMP [electromagnetic pulse] hardening against high-altitude nuclear detonation, encryption that requires a great deal of onboard computing power, protective devices for optics and things that aren't necessarily a part of the commercial sector. And sometimes there is some reason for that.

But we also need to understand, as Mr. Faga has indicated, and as the chairman has noted, and I think Dr. Hamre mentioned as well, there is robustness and resilience in having a lot of nodes, a lot of perhaps less capable assets.

And so there has—we are beginning to see a cultural change on the DOD side where they are understanding that that last ounce of weight doesn't necessarily need to go to one more diopter of capability. Maybe it needs to go to bolting on the little sensor that we all have outside our garage that turns the light on when somebody approaches so that we know when another satellite comes within—comes within our area. And, you know, and again, that is very simplistic, and believe me, I am not a satellite designer, but it shows you the kind of trades we need to make.

Maybe we take a little less capability and a lot more resilience as we move forward and at the same time draw much more heavily on the capabilities that are resonant in the commercial sector.

Mr. LAMBORN. Like so CubeSats [miniaturized satellites], for instance?

Admiral ELLIS. Right.

Dr. HAMRE. Sir, a friend of mine once said, you know, a candle maker will never invent electricity. And so we have done such a

brilliant job building satellites in the military we don't think anybody else knows how to do that.

You know, I doubt anybody inside the military DOD environment
would figure out how to land a rocket booster tail-first back on the
launch pad, you know? But the private sector did.

Now, it just seems to me we need to break out of the tyranny
of thinking we are the only people that know what we are doing.
There is a heck of a lot of people in the private sector now building
sophisticated platforms and we don't pay attention to what they
are doing. I mean, they are launching satellites where 10 people
can maintain that satellite.

Mr. LAMBORN. I had one provider, private outfit say that they
could put up CubeSats, very rudimentary but effective, not for six
figures or seven figures, but for five figures.

Dr. HAMRE. Yes.

Mr. LAMBORN. I yield back.

Mr. ROGERS. I thank the gentleman.

The Chair now recognizes the gentleman from Nebraska, Mr.
Ashford, for 5 minutes.

Mr. ASHFORD. Thank you. It is good to see you again. Admiral
Ellis is—still remains a legend in Omaha and thanks for all—certainly your service in commanding the strategic forces, but also in
your leadership in the community in so many things that you did
during your years there. So thank you.

And I also thank the rest of you for your service as well. It—
serving in Omaha is just a special——

[Laughter.]

Mr. ROGERS. It is a hardship.

Mr. ASHFORD. But it is a hardship, though.

[Laughter.]

Don't anybody repeat. But anyway——

[Laughter.]

I was going to follow on just a bit with Congressman Lamborn's
questions, and I think it was we have had other discussions about
other challenges and the need to—that perfection is the enemy of
good and that we need to find a quicker way to get to market or
get to the line with what we are doing. And I think Senator
Lamborn pretty well asked that question.

I have sort of a general question, though of Admiral Ellis, if I
could? When you were at strategic force, when you were the commander at that time, it was a time of great change. I mean, there
were things happening very quickly. There was operational change
going on and you were—oversaw that and admirably so.

Looking at today 10 years, 12 years later, where it's different
challenges, different threats, but how would you compare the two?
Over the last 12 years' times—we need the change we are talking
about here, but what are those differences that make this so critical at this time?

Admiral ELLIS. Well, as we have discussed all along, Mr. Ashford, and you know this very well, what has unfolded over the last
decade and a half is truly remarkable in the national security environment and you gentlemen and ladies live that every day and so
you know what I am about to say.

You know, the levels of threat that we have had to deal with, and not whipsawing but moving from the focus on classic Cold War-level adversarial relationships to the counterterrorism fight. It has changed the complexion and the context of the conversation in this Nation.

I was telling John before we convened, my son, believe it or not, is in the U.S. Army, graduated from West Point of all things, and he has done 19 deployments to Afghanistan in his career. And so my point here is this Nation has been fundamentally redirected and now the pendulum seems to be coming back.

We are seeing once again, you know, recidivist Russia and a China that is still trying to decide what it wants to be in terms of relationships as a great power.

And so there have been, in fairness, a lot of changes that have unfolded in the national security environment since I was privileged to wear the cloths of the Nation in Omaha up until 2004.

And that doesn't mean that I have got all the answers, that anyone does, but well, I think we need to be reminded by all of this that you can't design a perfect solution. That we need to design forces and capabilities in the context of this hearing that can serve all dimensions of national security.

And as I said in my prepared remarks, national security space is now redefined, as the ranking member indicated, to include the commercial elements and the economic. I mean, your cellphones won't work without out that timing signal.

It is not just your, the GPS on your golf cart. It is fundamental banking and other services. And so this is a new environment. We could have seen it coming. I believe that some people did see it coming looking at the reports of a decade and a half ago of commissions and panels.

But we are where we are, and the question is what do we do going forward and what kind of changes will be most effective and efficient in accomplishing what this Nation needs?

Mr. ASHFORD. Thank you, and it seems to me that that—and the changes are happening so much quicker now that designing the system to address it, it has to be flexible enough to, to Dr. Hamre's point, where we find private-public partnerships if, for lack of a better term, to get to that solution. So I don't know, Doctor, would you like to comment on that? Maybe it is not necessary, but if you——

Dr. HAMRE. Yes, sir. The private sector cannot afford to take 5 years or 8 years to develop a satellite. I mean, it—especially if you don't need to. So but we have, you know, in the Department, I mean, first of all, labor is a free good. Well, no wonder we have 700 people maintaining satellites. You don't pay for them.

But the private sector has to pay for every one of them and they cost money and so they have as few as they can. So they design reliability into the satellite.

I mean, we think about it in a different way in the private sector than—we have to start thinking differently. Candle makers have to start thinking in a different way.

Mr. ASHFORD. Thank you.

I yield back. Thanks, Mr. Chair.

Mr. ROGERS. Thank the gentleman.

The Chair now recognizes the gentleman from Oklahoma, Mr. Bridenstine, for 5 minutes.

Mr. BRIDENSTINE. Thank you, Mr. Chairman. I just wanted to quickly address I think a very intelligent question from Ranking Member Cooper. Dr. Hamre, I think you mentioned it as well, which is the cyber piece.

When you think about what satellites do, fundamentally they collect data. In some cases they create their own data. They transmit data. In some cases they process their own data onboard. So they are in essence just a component of the global network.

And so really you cannot separate space from cyberspace. They are one and the same and have to be thought about in that way. So I just wanted to make sure that I got that out there.

As I thought more about one of your suggestions, Dr. Hamre, regarding creating a U.S. Space Command, when you think about what the Department of Defense does in space it is my assessment, you know, we focus a lot on space support, which is launch and the satellite control network, those kind of activities.

We do space enhancements where we provide data to the war-fighter, whether it is communications or remote sensing, GPS signals. Those are all enhancements to the warfighter and/or for the Air Force for air dominance.

And then when you take it a step further, we are just now getting to the point where we as a country do space defense or space control, which I know in this town sometimes gets a reaction from people.

But ultimately, if we are going to be successful in fighting and winning in space we have to be able to use space and to deny our enemies from using space, which means we have to have some level of space control, which we as a nation have not even been thinking about until just recently.

So standing up, in my opinion, a U.S. Space Command when we are only now starting to think about space control, let alone delivering effects from space—when I am talking about effects I am talking about kinetic effects from space. Space is not at this point a deliverer of power projection.

That being the case, I think it might be premature to suggest that we need a U.S. Space Command kind of organization. It goes right back to what Admiral Ellis said. The challenge we have is in acquisition. And so I think it is important that when we think about that we focus on the defense space agency.

I think Dr. Hamre, you suggested it, and Admiral Ellis. Going back to the commercial, I had a NASA, former NASA Administrator Griffin in my office not too long ago, and he made a, I think, a very important point, which is right along the lines of what you are talking about, Dr. Hamre, which is he said the Department of the Navy is entirely dependent on fuel for ships, for airplanes. We need fuel.

But the Department of the Navy does not operate any drilling rigs. We don't do any refining of fuel. We actually buy fuel from the commercial sector.

When it comes to space and when it comes to communications, when it comes to remote sensing, we are moving in a direction where it is a commodity provided by the private sector.

So even the elements where we as a nation use space for fighting wars, space support, space enhancements, even those particular items are now being commercialized in ways that we haven't seen before, which means the Department of Defense needs to start focusing where it only can focus, which, of course, is in space control and eventually space warfare.

With that, Mr. Chairman, I will yield back.

Mr. ROGERS. I thank the gentleman.

I thank all the witnesses. We have been called for votes otherwise there would be a third round. But we have got 6 minutes to get over to the Capitol. I can't overstate how much I appreciate you and your thoughtfulness, your contributions to this dialogue. And I can't oveemphasize this is the beginning of the discussion that this committee is going to be having, not the end. And I thank you.

And with that we are adjourned.

[Whereupon, at 4:29 p.m., the subcommittee was adjourned.]

APPENDIX

SEPTEMBER 27, 2016

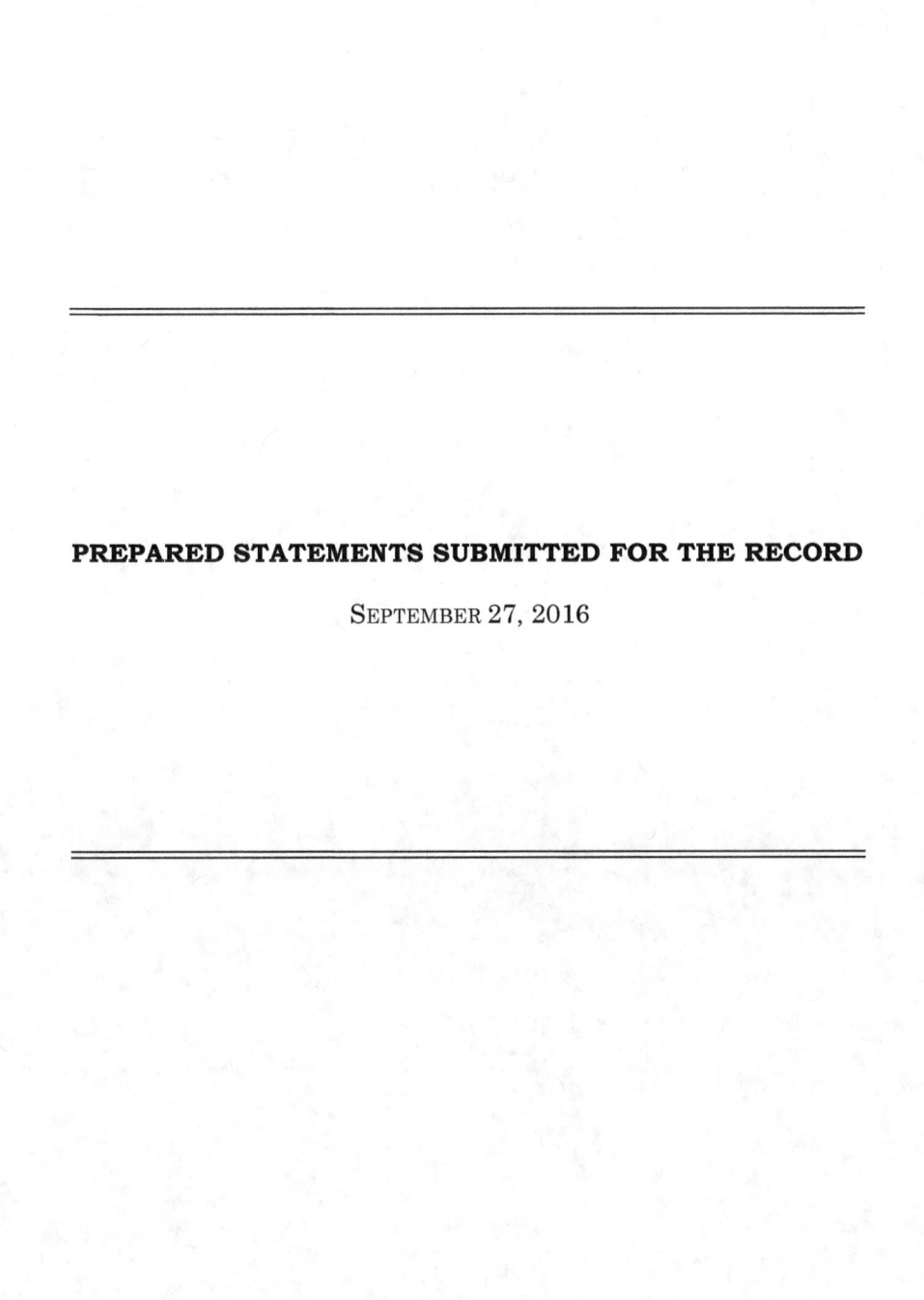

PREPARED STATEMENTS SUBMITTED FOR THE RECORD

SEPTEMBER 27, 2016

Opening Remarks
Honorable Michael D. Rogers
Chairman, Subcommittee on Strategic Forces
House Armed Services Committee

Hearing on National Security Space: 21st Century Challenges, 20th Century Organization

September 27, 2016

Good afternoon. I want to welcome everyone to the Strategic Forces Subcommittee's hearing on National Security Space: 21st Century Challenges, 20th Century Organization.

We are honored to have a distinguished panel of expert witnesses. We have:

Dr. John Hamre
Former Deputy Secretary of Defense

Retired Admiral James Ellis
Former Commander of U.S. Strategic Command

Mr. Martin Faga
Former Director of the National Reconnaissance Office and Assistant Secretary of the Air Force for Space.

Dr. Hamre, you are respected on both sides the political aisle, and known to be a wise and thoughtful leader on defense issues. I am aware that you have been studying space issues with a group of experts for some time. I am grateful to see you engaging on this very important subject.

Admiral Ellis and Mr. Faga, your leadership in national security space during your careers, as well as your recent co-chairing of the National Academies study on Space Defense and Protection, will provide this committee a very informed view regarding today's issues.

So why are we here today? I'd like to start with a quote.

> "It is not sufficient to have just resources, dollars, and weapons systems; we must also have an organization which will allow us to develop the proper strategy, necessary planning, and the full warfighting capability.
>
> We do not have an adequate organization structure today.
>
> We have made improvements, [but those] improvements have only been made at the margin; we need to do much more ... to be able to fight in today's environment ... [it] will require the concerted efforts of all four services. The services can't operate alone ... we are basically a committee system ... committees are very good in a

deliberative process, but they are notoriously poor in trying to run things."

This statement rings true for today's hearing. In fact, those words were spoken in this very same hearing room, by a person sitting in the very same seat as our witnesses are sitting in today.

However, that statement was made by a witness on February 3, 1982.

That witness was the Chairman of the Joint Chiefs of Staff, Air Force General David Jones, speaking about the organization of the Joint Staff.

The statement General Jones made took great courage and upset many people in the Department of Defense at the time. Organizational change is hard, and unfortunately many people take it personally.

However, General Jones' candor with Congress led to one of the most sweeping and greatly-needed reforms of the DOD: the Goldwater-Nichols Department of Defense Reorganization Act of 1986.

Just as General Jones had the courage to talk honestly with this committee, I commend the witnesses today, who have the courage to discuss the challenges of the posture and organization of our national security space activities.

No one in this room needs to be convinced of the importance of space to national security. Space allows our warfighters to project power across the globe, and keep our homeland safe.

Unfortunately, potential adversaries have recognized this, and they are developing weapons to take away the advantages that we have built in space.

There is a fundamental question before us today: Is the Department of Defense strategically postured to effectively respond to these threats and to prioritize the changed space domain over the long-term?

It is all too clear to me that we are not.

There is no clear leadership of the military space domain below the Secretary of Defense. Yes, there is an advisor, councils, chiefs, directors, and even commanders. As the GAO states, "DOD space leadership responsibilities are fragmented".

While we certainly have great leaders within the space enterprise, the structure is set up such that far too many people are able to say "no" without consequence for the delay and cost they create. Those responsible for organizing, training, equipping, and the operational missions in national security space are not actually in charge.

As General Hyten told the Senate Armed Services Committee in his confirmation hearing last week,

"We are moving much slower in certain areas than our adversaries. We need our industry and our acquisition process to move faster."

I agree with General Hyten that we need to move faster, however I'm concerned with the performance I'm seeing today. For example, the GPS Next Generation Ground System program is currently going through Nunn-

McCurdy breach for massive cost overruns, including a delay of operational capability that is 5 years beyond what was originally planned.

And I would talk about the Air Force's mismanagement of the weather satellite program, but I don't want to be spitting mad the rest of the day.

Unfortunately, this is not a single point case and it raises questions on the current enterprise's ability to deliver the next generation of space systems to address the threat we face.

Separately, the military space activities are managed within conflicting priorities of each of the armed services. Many resisted the views of air power visionaries such as Brigadier General Billy Mitchell and General Henry "Hap" Arnold to have an independent Air Force, however very few will argue today with wisdom of their vision.

We have the best military and civilian space professionals, alongside the most talented industry in the world. I believe the question is not of their ability, but rather what tools, structures, incentives, responsibilities and authority we need to give them to succeed. Put another way; even the best leaders can't succeed in a failed system.

For those that shy away from reform, I ask if it is better to wait for a crisis to motivate those to change, or to instead build a better system in a thoughtful and deliberate manner in order to avert such a crisis in the future? As Dr. Hamre foreshadows in his statement for the record: "space systems will be attacked".

The 9/11 Commission noted that we had all the information and people needed to prevent that days' events. We suffered from "a failure of imagination". We must resist the temptation of bureaucrats to wait for a disaster to fix this known failure. We must expect better. This committee will.

This hearing is the start of focused oversight that we will conduct on this important topic. I anticipate it will lead to major reform in the Fiscal Year 2018 National Defense Authorization Act.

I thank the witnesses again for being with us today, and I look forward to your testimony and discussion.

Opening Statement of Ranking Member Jim Cooper (TN-5)
National Security Space: 21st Century Challenges, 20th Century Organization
Subcommittee on Strategic Forces
Tuesday, September 27, 2016

Thank you, Mr. Chairman, for calling this panel of wise men to advise us on the best way to restructure America's military space programs. This is a timely response to the GAO's July 27, 2016 Report and to the National Academy of Science's August, 2016 Report.

I haven't made up my mind on whether we need to go beyond DOD's recent upgrading of the Secretary of the Air Force to also be the Principal Deputy Space Advisor, but three principles seem to be useful guides at a time like this:

1. **Don't reform a reform, particularly at the end of an eight-year presidential term.** Shouldn't we give the PDSA reform a chance to work, perhaps incentivizing the Secretary to do a particularly good job knowing that she is being carefully scrutinized? And, given the transition to a new administration and well-known congressional inertia, shouldn't we acknowledge that she will have many months before bolder reforms could be passed into law?

2. **If it ain't broke, don't fix it.** Most analyses indicate that the NRO, while not perfect, is doing an enviable job of serving its mission. That means that we should not jeopardize the NRO's current success with bureaucratic changes. If anything, we should learn from the NRO's success and share those best practices with other stakeholders of America's space assets.

3. **Instead of blank-slate reforms, who can fix today's problems?** Ideal organizations are fun to think about, but who can tell us how to fix problems like the 11-year delay on ground stations for our GPS satellite with advanced anti-jam capabilities, or the 5-year delay in the Next Generation Operational Control System, or the inability of DOD to coordinate with NOAA on weather satellites, or the possible duplication of effort between the Navy's MUOS and the Air Force's WGS satellites?

While we are considering major reforms, I suggest that we also consider reforms in personnel systems so that key positions can be held for much longer than the usual tour of duty. Key national assets should be supervised by people who have a long-term stake in the success of those systems, not in punching their ticket for their next promotion.

Thank you, Mr. Chairman. I look forward to the testimony of the witnesses.

Hearing before the
Subcommittee on Strategic Forces
Committee on Armed Services
United States House of Representatives

"NATIONAL SECURITY SPACE: 21ST CENTURY CHALLENGES, 20TH CENTURY ORGANIZATION"

Testimony by
John J. Hamre, Ph.D.
President and CEO
Center for Strategic and International Studies
Washington, D.C.

September 27, 20016

Chairman Rogers, Ranking Member Cooper, distinguished members of the Subcommittee on Strategic Forces, I am honored to be invited to appear today before the Strategic Forces Subcommittee, and to appear with my esteemed colleagues, Admiral James Ellis, former Commander-in-Chief of the U.S. Strategic Command, and Marty Faga, former head of the National Reconnaissance Office. There have been no finer leaders for American security than Jim Ellis and Marty Faga. It is a privilege to appear again before this Subcommittee. Your work on behalf of the American people is essential, and I commend you for holding this very important hearing today.

You have asked that we focus on "the challenges we face in the national security space domain and how these challenges relate to the organization and management, leadership structure, acquisition process, operational authorities" for the space mission. I will focus more on the challenges we face and offer a set of recommendations.

First, let me say that I am appearing here today as a private citizen. I am not representing the Center for Strategic and International Studies where I am the president and CEO. CSIS does not take positions on policy matters. Our boards and commissions do, but CSIS does not. So I am appearing here today in a private capacity.

I know that our time is brief, so I will focus briefly on 10 propositions. I would be pleased to amplify on any of these propositions during the question and answer period.

First, we once could count on assured use of space-based resources for any operational mission for the Department of Defense and the intelligence community. That is no longer the case. Adversaries have moved aggressively to create capabilities to challenge our use of space. It is a serious threat, and very real.

Second, we have good broad space policy guidelines. But those space policy guidelines are not accompanied by sufficient operational planning when it comes to continuity of operations. We lack the redundancy and capacity to reconstitute space resources in the event of a dedicated attack. More importantly, there is no operational doctrine concerning defending space or responding to imminent threat against space resources. The scale of vulnerability is great, and the detailed assessment and operational planning required to ameliorate these vulnerabilities is insufficient.

Third, space systems will be attacked (and this includes the elements of the system on the ground). Indeed, the first strike in a conventional war could well be in space. We have not devoted adequate time and focus on what it takes to operate space systems in a contested environment.

Fourth, the passage of time gives us options that we did not have in the last century. The huge expansion of commercial activity in space, and the internationalization of commercial space activity, are opportunities not just threats.

Fifth, perhaps the greatest near term threat we face is the vulnerability of our space systems—satellites yes, but certainly ground-based support systems—to cyber disruption. Cyber-attack is the most powerful step an adversary can take without triggering a redline to war. We have seen public displays of Russia's hacking capabilities. We must assume they are already inside important space IT systems. The Secretary should immediately launch an assurance review of space control systems. The space command and control architecture must be mapped to exquisite detail and a vulnerability assessment must be undertaken.

Sixth, while individual combatant commanders may anticipate some disruption, none of them has fully anticipated the impact on their plans of a robust attack on space systems (here used generically to refer to on-orbit and terrestrial elements). We need to stress-test our war plans. I would give this assignment to the Chairman of the Joint Chiefs of Staff and ask him to report back next year on his findings.

Seventh, every incoming Administration conducts a fundamental review of the policies, budgets and problems that they inherit. This is a time for making fundamental choices for at least the first four years of a presidency. After conducting the stress test, the next Secretary of Defense and the next Director of National Intelligence should establish a joint review committee to establish a vulnerability baseline for all space systems and assess the program-of-record to address these vulnerabilities. This is the time to get a proper balance between plans and resources.

Eight, our global positioning system is subject to jamming and could be attacked. We should plan now to install new chips in receiver units that allow that unit to receive the signals from all global positioning systems. There needs to be some care in implementing this, to be sure, but GPS is too critical for our war-fighting to have it jeopardized by hostile action.

Nine, as I mentioned earlier, the huge expansion of commercial space activity is an opportunity. I believe we should substantially shift our focus in space-based communications to rely on commercial platforms, including foreign satellites. Redundancy is the key and we need many more channels to insure continued communication links.

Ten, I believe we should start now to diversify our remote sensing systems. I use the term remote sensing to encompass all of our reconnaissance platforms. We still need high fidelity systems, to be sure. But we cannot count on their assured continued operation in time of combat. So we need to diversify our capabilities through hosted payloads on other satellite platforms.

Organizing for Space

Now let me come to the point of your hearing, which is the role that leadership and organization plays in our space program. I have spent a good deal of time talking this through with colleagues who are far more knowledgeable than am I about space. Honestly, there is no consensus on the way forward. We are not well organized to deal with the new challenges we face in space. The old structure may have been sufficient when space was an uncontested area of operations. That time has passed.

I have discussed several broad options with my colleagues who do specialize in the space mission. It seems to me we have four alternatives

Alternative 1: Create a 5th military service, a Space Service
Alternative 2: Elevate the Space Command to become a Unified command on par with the Strategic Command and other combatant commands
Alternative 3: Establish the space mission along the lines of the Missile Defense Agency, as a unified agency with a focused mission reporting directly to the Secretary of Defense.
Alternative 4: Model a new relationship for space analogous to the Department of Navy which has a Navy and a Marine Corps. In this instance, a Space Service would be established within the Department of the Air Force, but with separate budgets, career management, etc.

As I stated earlier, there is no consensus among my space expert friends on which alternative we should pursue. I have spent a lot of time studying the organization of the Department of Defense. Every organizational question comes down to "moats and gates". Organizations naturally define borders for themselves and build bureaucratic moats to protect those borders. And because of the complex and integrated way we must now fight wars, the Secretary has to find ways to build bridges across the moats.

For various reasons, I would advocate elevating the Space Command to become equal in stature to the Strategic Command, as a joint war-fighting unified command. I think all of the other options make the moat too wide and the gates/bridges too few. We know how to work with unified commands in the joint command system. If you feel we need to beef up the capabilities of that command, we can always add the exceptional budgeting and acquisition procedures we use currently for the Special Forces Command.

I used to be the Comptroller for the Department of Defense. Honestly, I don't like carving out and giving exceptional budget controls to sub-elements of the Department of Defense. We have too little money in general to operate the Defense Department and the Secretary needs maximum flexibility to allocate resources where he believes they are most needed for the array of missions he faces. Therefore, as a matter of principle, I resist carving out exceptional budgetary authorities. But I also have to admit that the space mission is in danger, and we need exceptional efforts at this critical time.

Conclusion

Chairman Rogers, Ranking Member Cooper, distinguished members of the Subcommittee, I thank you for holding this very important hearing, and for inviting me to be a part of it. There is no single area in the Defense Department that has me more worried than the resiliency of our space assets. I am grateful that you are devoting so much time to this critical question. I would be pleased to answer any questions you might have for me.

John J. Hamre
CSIS President and CEO

John Hamre was elected president and CEO of CSIS in January 2000. Before joining CSIS, he served as the 26th U.S. deputy secretary of defense. Prior to holding that post, he was the under secretary of defense (comptroller) from 1993 to 1997. As comptroller, Dr. Hamre was the principal assistant to the secretary of defense for the preparation, presentation, and execution of the defense budget and management improvement programs. In 2007, Secretary of Defense Robert Gates appointed Dr. Hamre to serve as chairman of the Defense Policy Board.

Before serving in the Department of Defense, Dr. Hamre worked for 10 years as a professional staff member of the Senate Armed Services Committee. During that time, he was primarily responsible for the oversight and evaluation of procurement, research, and development programs, defense budget issues, and relations with the Senate Appropriations Committee. From 1978 to 1984, Dr. Hamre served in the Congressional Budget Office, where he became its deputy assistant director for national security and international affairs. In that position, he oversaw analysis and other support for committees in both the House of Representatives and the Senate. Dr. Hamre received his Ph.D., with distinction, in 1978 from the School of Advanced International Studies at Johns Hopkins University in Washington, D.C., where his studies focused on international politics and economics and U.S. foreign policy. In 1972, he received his B.A., with high distinction, from Augustana College in Sioux Falls, South Dakota, emphasizing political science and economics. The following year he studied as a Rockefeller fellow at the Harvard Divinity School in Cambridge, Massachusetts.

DISCLOSURE FORM FOR WITNESSES
COMMITTEE ON ARMED SERVICES
U.S. HOUSE OF REPRESENTATIVES

INSTRUCTION TO WITNESSES: Rule 11, clause 2(g)(5), of the Rules of the U.S. House of Representatives for the 114th Congress requires nongovernmental witnesses appearing before House committees to include in their written statements a curriculum vitae and a disclosure of the amount and source of any federal contracts or grants (including subcontracts and subgrants), or contracts or payments originating with a foreign government, received during the current and two previous calendar years either by the witness or by an entity represented by the witness and related to the subject matter of the hearing. This form is intended to assist witnesses appearing before the House Committee on Armed Services in complying with the House rule. Please note that a copy of these statements, with appropriate redactions to protect the witness's personal privacy (including home address and phone number) will be made publicly available in electronic form not later than one day after the witness's appearance before the committee. Witnesses may list additional grants, contracts, or payments on additional sheets, if necessary.

Witness name: John J. Hamre

Capacity in which appearing: (check one)

● Individual

○ Representative

If appearing in a representative capacity, name of the company, association or other entity being represented: _____

Federal Contract or Grant Information: If you or the entity you represent before the Committee on Armed Services has contracts (including subcontracts) or grants (including subgrants) with the federal government, please provide the following information:

2015

Federal grant/ contract	Federal agency	Dollar value	Subject of contract or grant

2014

Federal grant/ contract	Federal agency	Dollar value	Subject of contract or grant

2013

Federal grant/ contract	Federal agency	Dollar value	Subject of contract or grant

Foreign Government Contract or Payment Information: If you or the entity you represent before the Committee on Armed Services has contracts or payments originating from a foreign government, please provide the following information:

2015

Foreign contract/ payment	Foreign government	Dollar value	Subject of contract or payment

2014

Foreign contract/ payment	Foreign government	Dollar value	Subject of contract or payment

2013

Foreign contract/ payment	Foreign government	Dollar value	Subject of contract or payment

Statement Before the

House Armed Services Subcommittee on Strategic Forces

"National Security Space: 21st Century Challenges, 20th Century Organization"

A Testimony by:

Admiral James O. Ellis, Jr., USN (Ret)

Former Commander, United States Strategic Command

September 27, 2016

2118 Rayburn House Office Building

Ellis: Testimony, House Armed Services Committee on Strategic Forces   09/27/2016

We set sail on this new sea because there is new knowledge to be gained, and new rights to be won, and they must be won and used for the progress of all people. For space science, like nuclear science and all technology, has no conscience of its own. Whether it will become a force for good or ill depends on man, and only if the United States occupies a position of pre-eminence can we help decide whether this new ocean will be a sea of peace or a new terrifying theater of war.

President John F. Kennedy
speech at Rice University
September 12, 1962

Chairman Rogers, Ranking Member Cooper, distinguished members of the Committee, thank you for your invitation to appear today to discuss the challenges confronting National Security Space assets, operations, and organizations. As the Committee is aware, I have been privileged over the past 18 months to co-chair a Congressionally-directed classified study by the National Academy of Science on National Security Space Protection and Defense. Both a classified and unclassified version of that study have been delivered to the Committee. While comprehensively addressing technological, policy, and strategy issues, the study results did not extend to organizational findings and recommendations and I appear at the invitation of the Subcommittee to present my own views on these critical issues, not those of the other study participants or the National Academy of Science.

As this Committee is well aware and as has now been widely acknowledged, the national security of the United States is inextricably linked to space and our unimpeded access to the capabilities resident in or traveling through that domain. Since the dawn of the Space Age, all those who have been a part of what was once a race between two superpowers and is now a $315 billion global enterprise, have implicitly understood this linkage. Over more than six decades, that reliance on space systems has deepened and broadened. What was once only a realm of exploration and national security has grown to include a commercial element that has become so ubiquitous that it has led us to fundamentally redefine the term national security space. President Kennedy was not the first to draw the analogy between space and the oceans of the world. The literature is sprinkled with references to space "ships," interplanetary "voyages," and star "fleets." Even the term "astronaut" is a combination of two Greek words, for "star" and "sailor." In many ways, the analogy is apt in that space exploration, initially, and exploitation, ultimately, have parallels in mankind's first tentative maritime endeavors. Sea-borne voyages of discovery led to the establishment of trade routes, colonial expansion, and, finally, contests for influence and security in the new domain.

The significant difference, of course, between the creation of global maritime policy and practice and that of the space domain is time. The technologies, customary behaviors, conventions and, eventually, treaties governing military and commercial naval activity evolved over centuries along with the enabling operational concepts, naval strategies, nation-states and attendant diplomacy. The system was thus able to gradually incorporate advances, slowly accommodate stresses, and, to some degree, resolve conflicts in a deliberate manner over time.

A key aspect of the space domain is that the speed of advances in access and space-borne capabilities has significantly outpaced the creation of guiding national -- let alone international -- strategies and policies. The technological advances in space systems an increased reliance on them have created a space-enabled "critical infrastructure" that has not been matched by coherent supporting protection and loss-mitigation strategies, clearly articulated and accepted policies, and robust defensive capabilities. These gaps have created newfound concern domestically, confusion on the part of allies, and opportunities for misalignment and misperceptions on the part of potential adversaries. The need to rapidly, precisely, and effectively address all of these factors has created an environment of urgency to find mitigation strategies, fill policy gaps, and fund new capabilities. Done poorly, rapid efforts and expansive rhetoric can exacerbate existing tensions, pursue capabilities that add only marginally to system security, and increase the probability of misunderstanding or miscalculation on the part of potential adversaries. Well-coordinated and properly executed, these efforts can meet real needs, add essential system security, and promote stability. These efforts must succeed. National security and global stability in space and on Earth demand it.

The Subcommittee, in its letter of invitation, asked that the witnesses address several specific issues related to the challenges we face in the national security space domain. Those included the organization, management, leadership structure, acquisition process, operational authorities and other associated elements of the space posture of the Department of Defense (DoD) and the National Reconnaissance Office (NRO). In preparing my response, I drew on my own experience and explored previous studies of the issue, some decades old, as well as a recent summary GAO report to Congress on the subject.

Before I continue, with your indulgence, I would make two points. First, my remarks in no way impugn the efforts of most of those who labor every day in support of our nation's national security space capabilities. Whether in or out of uniform, in government or the private sector, from the halls of the Pentagon and the tactical command centers to the industry factory floors and the launch complexes, they are among the most dedicated and skilled who serve our nation and have created a national security space capability that is the envy of the world. In many ways, they are as frustrated as we are and want the tools to be able to do even better. They know better than anyone that, in national security space, despite their efforts, we are not yet where we need to be. When we speak to them of change, rather than shy away from it, they ask the not-so-rhetorical question: "What are we waiting for?"

Second, we must remind ourselves that organizational change alone, in and of itself, though often an important factor, is rarely an effective stand-alone solution to a major problem. The reality is that every organization is sub-optimized for something, reflective of the tensions between speed, quality and cost as well as the difficult-to-discern differences between what you do the most and what is most important. An alternative approach is to simply make someone responsible, at a senior and impactful level, give them all the authority they need, and make them accountable for outcomes, not aspirations. If they successfully drive real change in outcomes, then, if organizational changes are necessary down the road, the form should follow function. If we get the "What, When and Why" right, the "How" will follow. Organizationally, I often note how the sidewalks should be placed on a college campus: where the paths are worn in the grass. That is the clearest indicator of how interaction really works, in practice, not in theory. In my view, we need not and should not try to precisely define a complex new architecture first. There is important work to be done now.

Ellis: Testimony, House Armed Services Committee on Strategic Forces   09/27/2016

"Any intelligent fool can make things bigger and more complex. It takes a touch of genius – and a lot of courage – to move in the opposite direction" —Albert Einstein

As this committee is aware, in a recent report to Congress, the General Accountability Office interviewed 17 long-serving space experts and surveyed over 20 years of critical assessments of national security space planning, acquisition and management. They distilled that down to four selected proposals for change that cover the full spectrum from, in naval parlance, "steady as she goes" to "hard right rudder." In the interest of time and to facilitate a consistent discussion, my remaining comments will focus on those choices.

No Further Changes: Allow time for the recent dual-hatting of the Secretary of the Air Force as Principal DoD Space Advisor (PDSA) to work.

While I appreciate the preeminent role of the US Air Force in space acquisition and operations and have great admiration and respect for Secretary James, I do not believe that this option goes far, or high, enough, no pun intended. We are nearly a year into the process so an assessment of progress should be possible. There are a many stakeholders in the DoD space arena, including all of the other services and the NRO, none of which are subordinate to the Air Force and all of which might question the true independence of a "first among equals" structure which gives a single service oversight of a DoD-wide program. Span-of-control is also an issue; I know how hard SECAF works Air Force issues; what is she delegating in order to take on this new and equally challenging responsibility? The "A" in PDSA is also a concern; an advisory role can be useful but the real leadership challenges come when consensus is not achieved and a decision and immediate action is still required. In the national security space environment, the need is urgent and the challenges are real.

Create a Space Acquisition Agency: Combine SMC and NRO.

I believe this solution would be far too narrow, neglect process, structural and cultural realities and risk "homogenizing" two very different organizations and, in so doing decrease the effectiveness of both. It is not clear which or whose procurement rules would apply and, if a new set needed to be established, risks beginning a process of space acquisition regulation creation that would be characterized by "3 L's": Loud, Legal and Long. I also value the healthy tension between two independent development and procurement entities. It mirrors, in a sense, the historic rivalry between the nation's nuclear laboratories where each took different and competitive approaches to solving shared problems. Creativity and innovation were encouraged and national security benefited as a result. Finally, space acquisition is a critical subset of a larger DoD acquisition process. Wholesale procurement reform should be pursued in the Department while making full use in the near-term of appropriate waivers, programmatic exceptions, innovative contract vehicles, delegated authorities, and other tools and demanding, as I noted earlier, full accountability for outcomes, not aspirations.

Create a Space Force: New military department for the space domain.

In my personal view, this is easily at once the most far-reaching and most disruptive of the postulated options. A new department and a new military service would be a decade in the making and drain and concentrate critical space expertise just reaching maturity in the DoD and, especially, that resident in the other services. It would risk centralizing and isolating space knowledge and skills, reversing two decades' worth of effort to get space understanding and employment down to the warfighter, no matter what service or agency they serve. The bureaucratic effort to create a new entity would be staggering: literally everything would need to be created anew, from policy, roles and missions to budgets, operational and training facilities and personnel support. The debate, distractions and decisions could be drawn-out over two administrations and five Congresses, with the potential for iterative alterations to the path and objectives. In this case, effectively simplifying and reforming the "devil we know" is a far better option.

"Perhaps because Americans as a nation have a gift for organizing, we tend to meet any new situation by reorganization, and a wonderful method it is for creating the illusion of progress at a mere cost of confusion, inefficiency and demoralization."

Charlton Ogburn Jr., The Marauders, Quote p. 60
Harper & Brothers, New York, 1959,

Creation of a Defense Space Agency: Combine military space functions into one agency but leave the NRO unchanged.

In my opinion, this concept addresses the essential requirements for driving real, timely and effective change in the oversight of US national security space. Properly constituted, it will clearly define the responsibilities, authorities and accountability, in other words, leadership, in a single entity for oversight of military space. After full stake-holder consultation, USD (Space) should also have full decision making authority, subject, of course, to Secretary of Defense review. Combining space acquisition functions of all military agencies into one organization, the NRO would remain a separate organization, which, as noted earlier, I fully support. As a DoD entity, however, the NRO would report to USD (Space) to ensure consistency of policy, cohesiveness of strategy and complementarity of capability. The concept, as the GAO noted, will provide a single leadership organization for all military space activities, provide greater unity and integration of military space acquisitions, and bring focused OSD-level oversight of military space policies and execution. Over a decade ago the Allard Commission on the Organization and Management of National Security Space forcefully noted as a central conclusion that "A strong executive is needed to integrate customer capability needs, set resource priorities, evaluate alternatives, develop and advocate investment plans and programs, and formulate and execute budgets for National Security Space. This executive must be responsive to DoD, the Intelligence Community, and other customers for Space capabilities, and must serve as a focal point for coordinating efforts across the federal government." As those space warfighters I referenced earlier asked: "What are we waiting for?"

Final Thoughts

Before concluding, there are several other points I would like to make:

(1) The technological advances in space systems and the world's increased reliance on them have created a space-enabled "critical infrastructure" that is an integral part of the national and global information infrastructure. This network includes both civilian

resources that are used in support of national security efforts and those that support more broadly economic and societal well-being around the world. National security space has been redefined and, as a result, must be addressed in a global context. An effective US response to growing space threats cannot be implemented solely by the national security space sector but requires a "whole of nation" response to include civil, commercial and international partnerships.

(2) A key aspect of national security space, as we now define it, is that the speed of advances in access to space and space-borne capabilities have significantly outpaced the creation of guiding national – let alone international – capabilities, strategies and policies. We have consistently underestimated both the rate of increase in our own space-related capabilities, our reliance on them, and the rate at which potential threats have progressed with the ability to counter them.

(3) When addressing a challenge, there is an understandable tendency to focus on the system details and operating procedures and neglect the essential broader context. I call it "working the technical and the tactical." We will always need a full and complete understanding of both what we are trying to do and what are the appropriate limits on what we are allowed to do. The truth is that clear and unambiguous civilian and senior military policy and strategy guidance are essential to ensuring we match resources with requirements to achieve unity of purpose and effectiveness of outcome. They are also critical to reassuring our allies and deterring potential adversaries. If we are to ensure space remains accessible and secure, we must continue to lead global efforts and be very clear about what we stand for and what we will not stand for in that domain. We must not confuse effort with outcome or technology with strategy. Tactical energy in a strategic vacuum is a recipe for disaster.

Conclusion

Members of the Subcommittee. Let me conclude by thanking you all for the opportunity to offer a few thoughts as you continue your important deliberations. As we are all aware, and as the GAO has noted, the Department of Defense has made real and significant progress in making national security space a national priority, a critical first step. Some limited progress has been made in four other areas highlighted as important in oversight and assessment reports dating back two decades. Where progress has not been verifiably made is in the last finding common to those reports: the need for unified leadership and authority in national security space. In my opinion, this is the single most important action to be taken. Given the appropriate resources and authorities, the right leader can dramatically improve the national security space environment we have and shape the environment we need.

I congratulate the Subcommittee for its interest in this critically important topic. I thank you for allowing me to contribute in a small way to your deliberations, and look forward to your questions.

53

"I do not say the we should or will go unprotected against the hostile misuse of space any more than we go unprotected against the hostile use of land or sea, but I do say that space can be explored and mastered without feeding the fires of war, without repeating the mistakes that man has made in extending his writ around this globe of ours"

President John F. Kennedy,
speech at Rice University,
September 12, 1962

James O. Ellis, Jr.
Admiral, U.S. Navy (Retired)

James O. Ellis, Jr. currently serves as an Annenberg Distinguished Fellow at the Hoover Institution at Stanford University where he is also an Adjunct Professor teaching in the School of Engineering. He retired as President and Chief Executive Officer of the Institute of Nuclear Power Operations (INPO), located in Atlanta, Georgia, on May 18, 2012.

INPO, sponsored by the commercial nuclear industry, is an independent, nonprofit organization whose mission is to promote the highest levels of safety and reliability—to promote excellence—in the operation of nuclear electric generating plants.

In 2004, Admiral Ellis completed a distinguished 39-year Navy career as Commander of the United States Strategic Command during a time of challenge and change. In this role, he was responsible for the global command and control of United States strategic and space forces, reporting directly to the Secretary of Defense.

A 1969 graduate of the U.S. Naval Academy, Admiral Ellis was designated a Naval aviator in 1971. His service as a Navy fighter pilot included tours with two fighter squadrons, and assignment as Commanding Officer of an F/A-18 strike/fighter squadron. In 1991, he assumed command of the USS Abraham Lincoln, a nuclear-powered aircraft carrier. After selection to Rear Admiral, in 1996 he served as a carrier battle group commander leading contingency response operations in the Taiwan Straits.

His shore assignments included senior military staff tours directing operations for the U.S. Atlantic Fleet and as Deputy Chief of Naval Operations (Plans, Policy, and Operations). He also served as Commander in Chief, U.S. Naval Forces, Europe and Commander in Chief, Allied Forces, Southern Europe during a time of historic NATO expansion and led United States and NATO forces in combat and humanitarian operations during the 1999 Kosovo crisis.

Mr. Ellis holds a master's degree in aerospace engineering from the Georgia Institute of Technology and, in 2005, was inducted into the school's Engineering Hall of Fame. He also has a master's degree in aeronautical systems from the University of West Florida. He completed United States Navy Nuclear Power Training and was qualified in the operation and maintenance of naval nuclear propulsion plants. He is a graduate of the Navy Test Pilot School, the Navy Fighter Weapons School (Top Gun) and the Senior Officer Program in National Security Strategy at Harvard University. In 2013, Mr. Ellis was elected to the National Academy of Engineering.

His personal awards include the Defense Distinguished Service Medal (three awards), Navy Distinguished Service Medal (two awards), Legion of Merit (four awards), Defense Meritorious Service Medal, Meritorious Service Medal (two awards), and the Navy Commendation Medal, as well as numerous campaign and service awards. He was presented the Order of Merit of the Republic of Hungary, the Star of Merit and Honor from the Greek Ministry of Defense and the Joint Forces Medal of Honor and the Grand Order of Merit of the Italian Republic.

Mr. Ellis currently serves on the board of directors of the Lockheed Martin Corporation, Dominion Resources and Level 3 Communications, where he is the non-executive Chairman of the Board. In 2009 he completed three years of service as a Presidential Appointee on the President's Intelligence Advisory Board and, in 2006, he was a member of the Military Advisory Panel to the Iraq Study Group.

DISCLOSURE FORM FOR WITNESSES
COMMITTEE ON ARMED SERVICES
U.S. HOUSE OF REPRESENTATIVES

INSTRUCTION TO WITNESSES: Rule 11, clause 2(g)(5), of the Rules of the U.S. House of Representatives for the 114th Congress requires nongovernmental witnesses appearing before House committees to include in their written statements a curriculum vitae and a disclosure of the amount and source of any federal contracts or grants (including subcontracts and subgrants), or contracts or payments originating with a foreign government, received during the current and two previous calendar years either by the witness or by an entity represented by the witness and related to the subject matter of the hearing. This form is intended to assist witnesses appearing before the House Committee on Armed Services in complying with the House rule. Please note that a copy of these statements, with appropriate redactions to protect the witness's personal privacy (including home address and phone number) will be made publicly available in electronic form not later than one day after the witness's appearance before the committee. Witnesses may list additional grants, contracts, or payments on additional sheets, if necessary.

Witness name: _James Q. Ellis, Jr._

Capacity in which appearing: (check one)

🔘 Individual

◯ Representative

If appearing in a representative capacity, name of the company, association or other entity being represented: _____

Federal Contract or Grant Information: If you or the entity you represent before the Committee on Armed Services has contracts (including subcontracts) or grants (including subgrants) with the federal government, please provide the following information:

2015

Federal grant/ contract	Federal agency	Dollar value	Subject of contract or grant

2014

Federal grant/contract	Federal agency	Dollar value	Subject of contract or grant

2013

Federal grant/contract	Federal agency	Dollar value	Subject of contract or grant

Foreign Government Contract or Payment Information: If you or the entity you represent before the Committee on Armed Services has contracts or payments originating from a foreign government, please provide the following information:

2015

Foreign contract/payment	Foreign government	Dollar value	Subject of contract or payment

2014

Foreign contract/ payment	Foreign government	Dollar value	Subject of contract or payment

2013

Foreign contract/ payment	Foreign government	Dollar value	Subject of contract or payment

Hearing before the
Subcommittee on Strategic Forces
Committee on Armed Services
United States House of Representatives

"NATIONAL SECURITY SPACE: 21ST CENTURY
CHALLENGES, 20TH CENTURY ORGANIZATION"

Testimony of
Martin Faga
Former Director of the NRO
Former Assistant Secretary of the Air Force (Space)

September 27, 2016

Chairman Rogers, Ranking Member Cooper, and members of the Subcommittee, it is a pleasure to appear today to discuss the challenges confronting National Security Space assets, operations, and organizations. I served with ADM Ellis as a co-chair of the National Research Council study on Space Defense and Protection which this Committee chartered, and I will comment from time to time from the study but I come today in my personal capacity. In that regard, I bring a range of experience gained over several decades of involvement in the space field as a government official, company executive and corporate director. This includes service as Director of the NRO during the first Gulf War sometimes called the first space war and certainly the first major conflict in which space assets including NRO systems played an important role at the tactical level.

The Subcommittee itself and my colleagues have developed well the point that space has become so important that our adversaries fully understand the advantage to them to deny those capabilities to us. Several nations routinely demonstrate impressive capabilities clearly intended for us to see. They see the opportunity expressed by Sun Tzu 2500 years ago: *The supreme art of war is to subdue the enemy without fighting.* We can't allow that to happen.

For a view of just how important space it to modern combat capability, I was struck by the statement a few years ago by Army Lieutenant General Richard Formica who said, "every company commander depends on space, and takes it for granted." He was saying that dependence on space begins at the first level of command, the Captain who commands just over 100 soldiers.

Today, our discussion of response to these threats to space systems is termed resilience. That term tends to conjure up thoughts of hardened satellites making quick maneuvers in space to avoid attacking missiles. That is a view that is too narrow. The attack might well be by means of attack by jamming, cyber or laser. We need to think of the problem as one of mission assurance. That is, assuring that the mission currently assigned to a space system, for example communications, is provided in conflict and that may include non-space backup, switch to commercial satellites or other means.

I know that my colleagues will develop the organizational issues that you raised in your invitational letter. While I will comment on those issues, I'd like to do it from the perspective of acquisition which is a key component of the challenges that confront us.

During the conduct of the NRC study, we recognized that operating in an era where our presence in space will be challenged, requires that acquisition to acquire, modify, backup or replace space capability must be more flexible and more rapid than today. In current times, an analysis of alternatives takes two years to complete. At the end of that time, it commonly recommends continuation of the current system with little change. Gen. Hyten has recently complained that sometimes the underlying data presented in the AOA suggest substantial change that would improve resilience but that information is not carried through to the recommendation. When the authors were asked why, they replied that they received no requirements for resilience so they didn't know how to treat it. This is not a desirable answer but an understandable one. The Combatant Commands are only beginning to study and understand their needs for resilience

including backups and they have few tools for simulation and analysis that would help them like the robust tools that exist for analysis of ground, air or naval combat
Once requirements are set and programs underway, we know that they take far longer to accomplish than they should and that we can tolerate in this era of contested space.

Programs are accomplished by Program Managers. They are my favorite and most admired people. When I was Director at NRO, we had about a dozen Program Managers among about 3000 total people, most of whom worked for those PMs. A point I repeatedly made was "Program Managers are the most important people in the organization and the job of all of the rest of us, including me, is to support them in getting their job done". I hope the Director would say the same thing today.

That is not the life of a Program Manager in DoD today. In its recent report on Defense Space Acquisitions, the GAO noted that for some programs, PMs are reviewed by 56 organizations at 8 levels above the PM. Needless to say these long processes consume months and much of the time and energy of the PM who I would like to see managing his program, interacting with his staff, his contractors, and his ultimate users. Moreover, in a recent conversation with a PM for a mid-sized program, he related that he had been through all of the steps to appear before the Under Secretary for AT&L but the Secretary has a very busy schedule and his appointment is several months away. I asked what he was doing in the interim. He replied, "wait." I will return to this point later.

PM authorities today are often tempered by "permissions." If I ask a PM whether he has the authority to do a particular thing, he is likely to reply, "yes, but I don't have permission." What he means is that levels above him have required that before he exercise authorities previously granted, that he receive their permission. This effectively removes authority thought to be granted.

When I watch the life of Program Managers today, I am reminded of a statement made by President Theodore Roosevelt in 1908:

"It is not the critic who counts,
 not the man who points out how the strong man stumbled,
or where the doer of deeds could have done them better.

The credit belongs to the man who is actually in the arena;
whose face is marred by dust and sweat and blood;
who strives valiantly;
who errs and comes short again and again;
who knows the great enthusiasms, the great devotions,
and spends himself in a worthy cause;

who, at the best, knows in the end the triumph of high achievement;
 and who, at the worst, if he fails, at least fails while daring greatly,
 so that his place shall never be with those cold and
timid souls who know neither victory or defeat."

Men in the arena have accomplished great things for our country including fleets of space systems that are the envy of the world. That's why people want to have the ability to attack them.

In it's report, the GAO also stated, "By contrast, the NRO's processes appear more streamlined than DOD's." Why is that? There are a number of reasons:

-The NRO has a relatively narrow mission whose high priority is widely acknowledged.

-The NRO is a joint activity of the DNI and the SecDef and the Director reports to them through a very short reporting chain. This joint activity arrangement of the last 50+ years is unusual but not unique. Another example is Naval Reactors which a joint activity of the Navy and the Department of Energy and is also very successful.

-The NRO can engage fully in the budget process of which it is a part. It would be unusual for significant pieces of NRO budget to mysteriously disappear as happens frequently to DoD PMs.

-The NRO is subject to reasonable oversight, although greatly increased in recent years.

-The NRO must and does follow the Federal Acquisition Regulations but not all of the DoD supplments.

-The NRO is an intelligence organization and understands that acquisition of reconnaissance satellites is only a means to an intelligence end. This means that NRO personnel are engaged with the Intelligence Community every day learning of their needs, offering assistance with the application of current systems and developing new concepts in company with their users.

-The NRO has a relatively small and highly capable staff. They're not alone. Naval Research Lab, many elements of NASA, Naval Reactors, the S&T element of CIA among others are examples of organizations that enjoy very strong staff.

-"Decision Rights" are reasonably clear within the NRO. Decision Rights is the concept that each person knows what decisions they can make and are expected to make and knows when to ask upward or delegate downward.

-Work at the NRO is exciting, challenging and rewarding. People are charged up about their work, something I have witnessed there within the last two weeks.

In addition to DoD and NRO space activities, there is a third element that needs to be mentioned. That is commercial space systems with national security application. Today, that is primarily satellite imaging and communications. The DoD buys lots of commercial satcom but often with short term contracts or on the spot market meaning to buy today what you need today but that means if it is available and also usually means at premium price. For years, Satcom operators have pushed the government to engage in longer term arrangements that might involve entire satellites for their entire lifetime thus spurring investment in capabilities tightly tied to DoD needs.

There is an example of where the government did exactly this and it is in satellite imaging. NGA has a ten year, fixed price contract with DigitalGlobe to deliver imagery as a service. This meant that DigitalGlobe capitalized the satellites, had them built, launched them and operates them. NGA is entitled to a substantial portion of the capacity which, as a very large customer, it gets at a substantial discount from the normal commercial price. The imagery is simply delivered by cable to NGA servers every day. Pretty neat- avoid all of the acquisition complexities and just buy the service. Of course, this approach isn't applicable for systems with unique military needs and roles like Space Based Infrared System and others.

I'll close by offering some thoughts on organization. Ideas have been forth for many years of ways to organize space more effectively, to put one person in charge, to streamline, etc. We need to remember that acquisition of national security space systems is carried out almost entirely by three organizations: Air Force Space and Missile Systems Center, NRO and Navy's Space and Naval Warfare Systems Command. All are relatively small and capable organizations that work effectively with and on behalf of their users. Operations are carried out effectively by Air Force Space Command and smaller Navy and Army commands. The problem is the 56 organizations and 8 levels that the GAO described that sit above all of this. One common prescription is to establish a very senior position charged to pull it together. I worry that instead of solving the problem, we simply increase 56 organizations to 57. Moreover, space is a means to an end-military and intelligence capability. In my experience, the most important thing is to keep the acquisition process tightly tied to the mission, that is, the ultimate users.

One idea is to have an Under Secretary for Space and to have all national security space elements report to it. For the NRO, that means unplugging from the Under Secretary for Intelligence where it now reports and connect to another official at the same level. But, NRO is an intelligence agency and that's where it needs to be focused. I think similar arguments can be made for the military space acquisition elements that are connected to their operational commands.

Big organizational change comes with long term impacts. In 1992, I reorganized the NRO from an organization based on agency-Air Force, CIA and Navy- to one based on Intelligence function-Imagery and Signals Intelligence. I believed then and believe now that it was the right thing to do but it was wrenching change for the NRO for the next 10 years. In our current situation, I would start by asking the Secretary of Defense to review what all of the DoD parties involved with space do, and whether each is adding value. Are all participants really needed and can the DoD guidance, policy, budget and oversight processes be streamlined? The answer for some will be that their role is congressionally mandated so change may well require legislation. I would measure the response by constantly examining what happens to the Program Manager. When the person who is actually getting the job done starts on the journey, what happens along the way? If the Program Manager's life gets better, then we're on the road to success.

Thank you for the opportunity to offer my views today. I look forward to your questions.

Martin C. Faga
Former President and Chief Executive Officer, MITRE Corporation

Martin Faga retired as president, chief executive officer of MITRE on June 30, 2006. He was a member of the MITRE Board of Trustees until 2012.

Before joining MITRE, Mr. Faga served from 1989 until 1993 as Assistant Secretary of the Air Force for Space, where he was responsible for overall supervision of Air Force space matters. At the same time, he served as Director of the National Reconnaissance Office (NRO), responsible to the secretary of defense and the Director of Central Intelligence for the development, acquisition and operation of all U.S. satellite reconnaissance programs.

Mr. Faga is a Fellow of the National Academy of Public Administration, and is a member of the Board of Directors of the Association of Former Intelligence Officers. He served from 2006-2009 on the President's Intelligence Advisory Board and was a member of the Public Interest Declassification Board from 2006 to 2014.

Mr. Faga serves on the Board of Directors of Orbital ATK, is Chairman of the Board of Thomson Reuters Special Services and is a Proxy Holder at Inmarsat Government. He served on the boards of Electronic Data Systems from 2006 to 2008, GeoEye from 2006 to 2013, and DigitalGlobe from 2013 to 2015.

Mr. Faga received master and bachelor of science degrees in electrical engineering from Lehigh University in 1964 and 1963.

DISCLOSURE FORM FOR WITNESSES
COMMITTEE ON ARMED SERVICES
U.S. HOUSE OF REPRESENTATIVES

INSTRUCTION TO WITNESSES: Rule 11, clause 2(g)(5), of the Rules of the U.S.
House of Representatives for the 114th Congress requires nongovernmental witnesses
appearing before House committees to include in their written statements a curriculum
vitae and a disclosure of the amount and source of any federal contracts or grants
(including subcontracts and subgrants), or contracts or payments originating with a
foreign government, received during the current and two previous calendar years either
by the witness or by an entity represented by the witness and related to the subject matter
of the hearing. This form is intended to assist witnesses appearing before the House
Committee on Armed Services in complying with the House rule. Please note that a copy
of these statements, with appropriate redactions to protect the witness's personal privacy
(including home address and phone number) will be made publicly available in electronic
form not later than one day after the witness's appearance before the committee.
Witnesses may list additional grants, contracts, or payments on additional sheets, if
necessary.

Witness name: Martin C. Faga

Capacity in which appearing: (check one)

◉ Individual

◯ Representative

**If appearing in a representative capacity, name of the company, association or other
entity being represented:** _____

Federal Contract or Grant Information: If you or the entity you represent before the
Committee on Armed Services has contracts (including subcontracts) or grants (including
subgrants) with the federal government, please provide the following information:

2015

Federal grant/ contract	Federal agency	Dollar value	Subject of contract or grant

2014

Federal grant/ contract	Federal agency	Dollar value	Subject of contract or grant

2013

Federal grant/ contract	Federal agency	Dollar value	Subject of contract or grant

Foreign Government Contract or Payment Information: If you or the entity you represent before the Committee on Armed Services has contracts or payments originating from a foreign government, please provide the following information:

2015

Foreign contract/ payment	Foreign government	Dollar value	Subject of contract or payment

2014

Foreign contract/ payment	Foreign government	Dollar value	Subject of contract or payment

2013

Foreign contract/ payment	Foreign government	Dollar value	Subject of contract or payment

DOCUMENTS SUBMITTED FOR THE RECORD

SEPTEMBER 27, 2016

Finding 1: DOD Space Acquisitions, Management, and Oversight Are Fragmented Across Approximately 60 Stakeholders[12]

DOD

Office of the Secretary of Defense
- Under Secretary of Defense for Acquisition, Technology, and Logistics
  - Assistant Secretary of Defense, Acquisition
  - Assistant Secretary of Defense, Research & Engineering
  - Deputy Assistant Secretary of Defense, Space, Strategic, & Intel Systems
  - Deputy Assistant Secretary of Defense, C3, Cyber, & Business Systems
  - Performance Assessments & Root Cause Analyses
- Under Secretary of Defense for Intelligence
- Under Secretary of Defense for Policy
  - Deputy Assistant Secretary of Defense, Space Policy
- Under Secretary of Defense (Comptroller)/Chief Financial Officer
  - Director, Cost Assessment and Program Evaluation
  - Director, Operational Test and Evaluation
- Chief Information Officer
  - Defense Information Systems Agency

Joint Chiefs of Staff

Secretary of the Air Force/ Principal DOD Space Advisor
- Assistant Secretary of the Air Force, Acquisition
  - Deputy Assistant Secretary of the Air Force, Directorate of Space Programs
  - Program Executive Officer, Space
- Deputy Under Secretary of the Air Force (Space)/Director, PDSA Staff
- Air Force Cost Analysis Agency
- Air Force Materiel Command
  - Air Force Research Laboratory
- Air Force Intelligence, Surveillance and Reconnaissance Agency
  - Air Force Technical Applications Center
- Air Force Space Command
  - Air Force Space and Missile Systems Center
  - 14th Air Force

Secretary of the Army
- Army Space and Missile Defense Command
  - Program Executive Office, Missiles and Space
  - Army Research Laboratory

DOD (continued)

Secretary of the Navy
- Assistant Secretary of the Navy for Research, Development and Acquisition
  - Office of the Chief of Naval Operations
  - Naval Research Laboratory
  - Program Executive Office, Space Systems
  - Office of Naval Research

U.S. Marine Corps, Plans, Policies and Operations

U.S. Strategic Command
- Joint Functional Component Command for Space

Defense Advanced Research Projects Agency

Defense Special Missile and Astronautics Center

Missile Defense Agency

Executive Office of the President

Office of Management and Budget

Office of Science and Technology Policy

National Security Council

Intelligence Community

Office of the Director of National Intelligence

Central Intelligence Agency

National Air and Space Intelligence Center

Defense Intelligence Agency

National Geospatial-Intelligence Agency

National Reconnaissance Office

National Security Agency

Civilian Community

Department of Commerce: National Oceanic and Atmospheric Administration

Department of Energy: Lawrence Livermore, Los Alamos, and Sandia National Laboratories

Department of State

Department of Transportation: Federal Aviation Administration

National Aeronautics and Space Administration

[12]Stakeholders are organizations that have a role and responsibility in defense space acquisition management or oversight, or are customers or users of defense space programs.

(69)

QUESTIONS SUBMITTED BY MEMBERS POST HEARING

September 27, 2016

QUESTIONS SUBMITTED BY MR. ROGERS

Mr. ROGERS. The NRO is a defense agency; however it is not statutorily defined as a combat support agency (CSA). In contrast, the Defense Intelligence Agency, National Security Agency, and National Geospatial-Intelligence Agency are all combat support agencies. As we prepare for a war to extend into space, is it time we think of the NRO as a combat support agency?

Dr. HAMRE. I am not an expert here, but I suspect that the NRO status was set year back when it was jointly supervised by the Defense Department and the Director of Central Intelligence, the predecessor to the Director for National Intelligence. I would need to check with expert friends, but I know that the NRO functions as a combat support agency. The NRO also has important non-defense intelligence missions, and I don't know if the designation would complicate any of that. From a defense standpoint, it would be a good thing to have them also included as a combat support agency. But I would need to defer to others to know if that would prove to be a problem for their other national missions.

Mr. ROGERS. GAO stated that there was a 10-year gap between the delivery of GPS satellites and user equipment. There have been similar issues with other space programs, such as Space-Based Infrared Systems (SBIRS) and its ground station, the Advanced Extremely High Frequency (AEHF) Satellite and its ground terminals. Why do these acquisition problems, regarding the poor synchronization of delivery of satellite, ground, and user terminals, keep reoccurring?

Dr. HAMRE. We have tended to split the various components of a space program into different program offices under different services. Because the GPS signal needs to be incorporated into hundreds of combat systems and platforms, it wasn't possible to give the task of ground based user equipment to the GPS program office. This tends to reflect a general problem we have in the Department for systems that have broad application that cross service lines. The only way to solve that is for the Office of the Secretary of Defense to do a better job insisting there is integration and coordination for such complex systems with such broad applicability within the Department.

Mr. ROGERS. Are you seeing innovation and long-term research and development planning in national security space programs? Why or why not?

Dr. HAMRE. We still have a very dynamic laboratory environment, in both the private sector and in government laboratories. What is lacking is the capacity to move innovative new ideas from laboratories into actual procurement programs. My personal view is that this difficulty in introducing innovative new ideas is the byproduct of the Packard Commission recommendations, which made the mechanics of acquisition more important than technology innovation. The Director for Defense Research and Engineering used to be the third most powerful position in the Department of Defense, and always drew exceptionally talented individuals with broad experience. We diminished this position with the Packard Commission implementation and made the mechanics of acquisition more important. We are now suffering from this unintended development. The 2017 NDAA makes a good step at fixing this, but there is much more that needs to be done.

Mr. ROGERS. What are your views on the Joint Interagency Combined Operations Center (JICSpOC)? What should the future of it be, and how should it compare with the Joint Space Operations Center (JSpOC)? Should we have two operations centers serving different functions?

Dr. HAMRE. I think it is good to have an interagency joint operations center, and it should be integrated with the Joint Space Operations Center. Often other departments or bureaus of the government fear being brought into DOD operations centers because they are afraid of the mass and momentum you see in DOD organizations. They feel they will be coopted by being a part of a DOD operations center. It may be that the JICSpOC is a compromise so that we could get interagency participation. The most important thing is to make sure they are working seamlessly together.

Mr. ROGERS. What arrangements should be in place between the DOD and the IC and various commercial companies regarding the U.S. Government's ability to task and use commercial satellites in crisis or wartime?

Dr. HAMRE. I would direct the Committee's attention to something called the Civil Reserve Air Fleet, or CRAF. CRAF has been in place for 40 years. In essence, U.S. commercial airline companies join the CRAF program. If an emergency comes up, we can call on those aircraft in the CRAF to change their schedules and start flying missions for the Department of Defense. We pay them for this, of course, but more importantly, the U.S. Government indemnifies the aircraft when they are on government missions. We have a similar arrangement for cellular communications during a national emergency. This is the formula for emergency mobilization of commercial space assets. More importantly, I think we should start placing regular work (communications, some reconnaissance, etc) with commercial satellite companies in peacetime. We need to broaden the network we use so that potential adversaries do not have a limited set of government satellites to attack. We want to force them to attack a broad range of capabilities in a very public way as part of our deterrent strategy.

Mr. ROGERS. The NRO is a defense agency; however it is not statutorily defined as a combat support agency (CSA). In contrast, the Defense Intelligence Agency, National Security Agency, and National Geospatial-Intelligence Agency are all combat support agencies. As we prepare for a war to extend into space, is it time we think of the NRO as a combat support agency?

Admiral ELLIS. As you know, the NRO is not an intelligence agency. It designs, builds, and operates the reconnaissance satellites of the United States government, and provides satellite intelligence to several government agencies, particularly signals intelligence (SIGINT) to the NSA, imagery intelligence (IMINT) to the NGA, and measurement and signature intelligence (MASINT) to the DIA.

The intelligence it provides is essential to enabling other agencies to successfully meet all of our national security needs, including combat support. While, in that sense, the NRO provides indirect combat support, that contribution is already fully understood and appreciated. Unless such a designation would significantly enhance the NRO's already high effectiveness, I do not see it as an urgent need.

Mr. ROGERS. GAO stated that there was a 10-year gap between the delivery of GPS satellites and user equipment. There have been similar issues with other space programs, such as Space-Based Infrared Systems (SBIRS) and its ground station, the Advanced Extremely High Frequency (AEHF) Satellite and its ground terminals. Why do these acquisition problems, regarding the poor synchronization of delivery of satellite, ground, and user terminals, keep reoccurring?

Admiral ELLIS. While I do not have specific current knowledge of each of the systems described, such delays are often a result of procurement processes that separate the procurement of the ground system from the on-orbit segment, attempt to capture efficiencies by using a common ground system for more than one satellite constellation, or, in order to reduce program costs, attempt to use existing ground systems for new satellites, only to find that they later have to replace aging ground segments in order to fully employ the new systems.

All of the above are well-recognized challenges for which there are existing programmatic management, resourcing and leadership solutions.

Mr. ROGERS. Are you seeing innovation and long-term research and development planning in national security space programs? Why or why not?

Admiral ELLIS. I am seeing such efforts in both the government and the private sector but I am concerned that the level of investment is insufficient to recapture lost ground as our overall investment in critical national security research and development has declined in recent years.

As I noted in my prepared remarks, we have been surprised by the rate of technological change in national security space, both in terms of our increased reliance on it and, even more critically, by the dramatic increase in the ability of potential adversaries to threaten it.

Finally, while R&D investment is essential, so is the ability to know where the need is largest and the potential positive impact the greatest. We need more effective tools for system-wide analysis to ensure we are focusing on what is most important.

Mr. ROGERS. What are your views on the Joint Interagency Combined Operations Center (JICSpOC)? What should the future of it be, and how should it compare with the Joint Space Operations Center (JSpOC)? Should we have two operations centers serving different functions?

Admiral ELLIS. The answer, as with many things, is "it depends." The stated purpose of the newly-created JICSPOC is for the military, Intelligence Community (IC), and commercial partners to craft concepts of operation and clarify who does what and how in the event of attacks on U.S. satellites. In my view, that describes a place where a much-needed series of simulations and exercises can take place to enhance understanding of the national security space interrelationships, define overlapping capabilities and, most importantly, identify gaps in the structure, authority, and accountability. I fully support such immediate interagency and commercial outreach efforts; they are long overdue.

On the other hand, I believe strongly in unity of command, authority and accountability. As I note often, collaboration is not the same as consensus; someone has to be in charge. This is particularly true in the national security space domain where challenges can manifest themselves quickly, sometimes at the speed of light.

I support the experimental character of the JICSPOC but agree that the lessons from its tests need to move quickly to a single command center, appropriately staffed by all stakeholders, with a clearly defined chain of command. They are not lessons learned just because we write them down; we actually have to learn them and things need to change as a result.

Mr. ROGERS. Does the National Reconnaissance Office (NRO), which is a part of the DOD, have the same acquisition and decision-making challenges the military space program does? Why or why not?

Admiral ELLIS. The NRO is a much smaller and streamlined organization and, while the acquisition and decision-making challenges it faces are the same as the military space program, the speed with which the NRO can respond to them is much greater, the access to key decision makers is much easier, and the oversight regulations and restrictions are far fewer. All of this equates to a more effective procurement process, more technological agility, and clearer lines of responsibility and accountability.

Mr. ROGERS. Has the DOD and DNI been able to maintain oversight of the NRO, while still empowering the Director? Why are the NRO acquisitions more streamlined than the military space programs?

Admiral ELLIS. The organizational relationships among the DOD, the DNI and the NRO remain strong and the NRO continues to effectively and efficiently support both agencies. There have been some candid discussions about operational control of NRO satellites in the context of achieving consistent policies and clear, responsive decision-making in time of potential crisis. This has resulted in the creation of the JICSPOC to simulate and evaluate potential challenges and solutions.

As in the answer to the question above, the NRO is physically a much smaller and streamlined organization and, while the acquisition and decision-making challenges it faces are the same as the military space program, the speed with which the NRO can respond to them is much greater, the access to key decision makers is much easier, and the oversight regulations and restrictions are far fewer. All of this equates to a more effective procurement process, more technological agility, and clearer lines of responsibility and accountability.

Mr. ROGERS. Your National Academies report talked about the need to clarify operational authorities for space. Can you expand on that? What is your view of unity of command versus unity of effort?

Admiral ELLIS. There have recently been some candid discussions about operational control of all national security satellites, including the NRO assets and those commercial communications satellites used for national security purposes, in the context of achieving consistent policies and clear, responsive decision-making in time of potential crisis. This is understandably, a complex technology, policy, and authority issue. In fairness, the discussion has arisen as a result of our appropriately re-defining the scope of "national security space" to include all of the spaceborne resources we employ and those on which we rely as a nation and with our global partners. It should not and must not be viewed as a "power grab" but rather as an acknowledgement of newly appreciated realities of the nature, capabilities, and speed of potential threats.

This has resulted in the creation of the JICSPOC to simulate and evaluate potential challenges and solutions and to craft concepts of operation and clarify who does what and how in the event of attacks on U.S. satellites. In my view, that describes a place where a much-needed series of simulations and exercises can take place to enhance understanding of the national security space interrelationships, define overlapping capabilities and, most importantly, identify gaps in the structure, authority, and accountability. I fully support such immediate interagency efforts; they are long overdue.

I support the experimental character of the JICSPOC but agree that the lessons from its tests need to move quickly to a single command center, appropriately staffed by all stakeholders, with a clearly defined chain of command. They are not lessons learned just because we write them down; we actually have to learn them and things need to change as a result.

On the other hand, I believe strongly in unity of command, authority and accountability. As I note often, collaboration is not the same as consensus; someone has to be in charge. This is particularly true in the national security space domain where challenges can manifest themselves quickly, sometimes at the speed of light.

Mr. ROGERS. You took control of U.S. Strategic Command when U.S. Space Command was merged with it. Can you give us your perspectives of that decision, why it happened, and what has changed since then?

Admiral ELLIS. The combining of United States Strategic Command and United States Space Command took place in the context of redefining the term "strategic" in support of national security. Rather than "strategic" referring, as it had for decades, to nuclear and nuclear-related systems, the meaning was more broadly and classically expanded to mean anything having global, national, and high-level influence or impact. Clearly, all space systems were a critical part of those capabilities and essential enablers to each leg of the newly-defined "New Triad." To meet the nation's defense goals in the 21st century, the first leg of the New Triad, the offensive strike leg, went beyond the Cold War triad of intercontinental ballistic missiles (ICBMs), submarine-launched ballistic missiles (SLBMs), and long-range nuclear-armed bombers. ICBMs, SLBMs, bombers and nuclear weapons would, of course, continue to play a vital role. However, they would be just part of the first leg of the New Triad, integrated with new non-nuclear strategic capabilities that strengthened the credibility of our offensive deterrence. The second leg of the New Triad required development and deployment of both active and passive defenses—a recognition that offensive capabilities alone may not deter aggression in the new security environment of the 21st century. Active and passive defenses will not be perfect. However, by denying or reducing the effectiveness of limited attacks, defenses can discourage attacks, provide new capabilities for managing crises, and provide insurance against the failure of traditional deterrence. The new domain of cyberspace was also included in the new STRATCOM responsibilities. The third leg of the New Triad was a responsive defense infrastructure. Since the end of the Cold War, the U.S. defense infrastructure has contracted and our nuclear infrastructure has atrophied. New approaches to development and procurement of new capabilities were intended to ensure that it would not take 20 years or more to field new generations of weapon systems.. The effectiveness of this New Triad depended upon command and control, intelligence, and adaptive planning. "Exquisite" intelligence on the intentions and capabilities of adversaries can permit timely adjustments to the force and improve the precision with which it can strike and defend. The ability to plan the employment of the strike and defense forces flexibly and rapidly will provide the U.S. with a significant advantage in managing crises, deterring attack and conducting military operations. Much of this capability is resident in or enhanced by our space systems. In my view, the consolidation was entirely appropriate and was implemented with the full collaboration and cooperation of U.S. Space Command. It reflected the reality that the space systems are not a stand-alone capability but have significant value if shaped by, supportive of, and integrated with the warfighting combatant commands through the efforts of U.S. Strategic Command. The many and varied national security challenges since the combination have reinforced the value of the "strategic" systems resident in a single command with clear authority and accountability.

Mr. ROGERS. What arrangements should be in place between the DOD and the IC and various commercial companies regarding the U.S. Government's ability to task and use commercial satellites in crisis or wartime?

Admiral ELLIS. The stated purpose of the newly-created JICSPOC is for the military, Intelligence Community (IC), and commercial partners to craft concepts of operation and clarify who does what and how in the event of attacks on U.S. satellites. In my view, that describes a place where a much-needed series of simulations and exercises can take place to enhance understanding of the national security space interrelationships, define overlapping capabilities and, most importantly, identify gaps in the structure, authority, and accountability. I fully support such immediate interagency and commercial outreach efforts; they are long overdue.

On the other hand, I believe strongly in unity of command, authority and accountability. As I note often, collaboration is not the same as consensus; someone has to be in charge. This is particularly true in the national security space domain where challenges can manifest themselves quickly, sometimes at the speed of light.

I support the experimental character of the JICSPOC but agree that the lessons from its tests need to move quickly to a single command center, appropriately staffed by all stakeholders, with a clearly defined chain of command. They are not lessons learned just because we write them down; we actually have to learn them and things need to change as a result.

Mr. ROGERS. The NRO is a defense agency; however it is not statutorily defined as a combat support agency (CSA). In contrast, the Defense Intelligence Agency, National Security Agency, and National Geospatial-Intelligence Agency are all combat support agencies. As we prepare for a war to extend into space, is it time we think of the NRO as a combat support agency?

Mr. FAGA. I don' think there is a need or value to designate NRO as a Combat Support Agency. Unlike DIA, NSA, NGA, NRO is a combined agency of the DOD and DNI. It receives its tasking direction from the functional managers who are acting on behalf of the DNI in that capacity. Further, NRO is something like a Military Service in that it develops, acquires and operates reconnaissance satellites but it makes no decisions about how those assets will be deployed. Accordingly, it is not in a position to take direct military tasking, but responds to tasking, including military tasking, through already established mechanisms which operate through the DNI.

Mr. ROGERS. GAO stated that there was a 10-year gap between the delivery of GPS satellites and user equipment. There have been similar issues with other space programs, such as Space-Based Infrared Systems (SBIRS) and its ground station, the Advanced Extremely High Frequency (AEHF) Satellite and its ground terminals. Why do these acquisition problems, regarding the poor synchronization of delivery of satellite, ground, and user terminals, keep reoccurring?

Mr. FAGA. Commonly, space systems and their ground or user equipment have been treated as separate activities, with separate budgeting and separate development organizations. For example, the Air Force develops the space segment at SMC/Los Angeles and the ground segment or user equipment at Electronic Systems Command/Boston. SMC is a part of AF Space Command and ESC now renamed as a part of the AF Life Cycle Management Center, is a part of Materiel Command. 1 Budgeting for the two is separate and largely independent. It is easy for space and ground to get badly out of sync and often did.

Mr. ROGERS. Are you seeing innovation and long-term research and development planning in national security space programs? Why or why not?

Mr. FAGA. Yes, and especially so since the concern for resiliency has arisen in the last couple of years. This concern has forced consideration of changes in architectures and in individual satellites as well as serious consideration of the best role for commercial offerings.

That said, during interviews held by the National Research Council team that produced NRC's report of Space Defense and Protection, space system contractors told us that NRO was more interested in innovations and AF more likely to buy more of the same. One consequence of that, the contractors reported, is that it is hard to develop good staff skills and experience if innovation isn't introduced regularly, to say nothing of the performance advantages typically obtained.

Mr. ROGERS. What are your views on the Joint Interagency Combined Operations Center (JICSpOC)? What should the future of it be, and how should it compare with the Joint Space Operations Center (JSpOC)? Should we have two operations centers serving different functions?

Mr. FAGA. I am not familiar in any detail with the JICSpOC but I believe the idea is that initially it will serve as a center to develop the systems and techniques to perform Space Situational Awareness at the pace necessary in a contested environment. Lt. Gen. Raymond, while service as Commander of 14th AF, explained that the JSpOC performs its tasks over periods of hours to days while future operations will have to do so in minutes, even seconds. The AF is learning how to do that at JICSpOC. Eventually, I believe that JICSpOC will take over the mission operationally and there will be one, vastly more capable center. It will take several years to achieve this.

Mr. ROGERS. Does the National Reconnaissance Office (NRO), which is a part of the DOD, have the same acquisition and decision-making challenges the military space program does? Why or why not?

Mr. FAGA. The NRO isn't simply "a part of the DOD" but is a joint activity of the DNI and the DOD. This is an important distinction because the NRO budget is largely controlled by the DNI as is operational tasking. DOD elements like NGA and NSA especially, play large roles in both but they do so in their capacity of support to the DNI. All of this means that the NRO carries out a relatively narrow mission, albeit important and expensive, for a limited user group with which it can interact intimately. Thus getting to decision is generally far easier than within DOD.

An additional factor affecting NRO is that it must follow the Federal Acquisition Regulations but not all of the Defense supplements which are voluminous. This long standing practice reflects the fact that the experience level of contracting personnel in NRO tends to be higher than in DOD and the greater flexibility granted by the FAR is appropriate when in the hands of a highly experienced contracts officer.

Mr. ROGERS. Has the DOD and DNI been able to maintain oversight of the NRO, while still empowering the Director? Why are the NRO acquisitions more streamlined than the military space programs?

Mr. FAGA. Yes. While DOD and DNI oversight is far more extensive than in earlier decades, the Director remains empowered. This is largely because she can interact at very senior levels with the DOD and ODNI and can make her case directly and receive direction and decisions quickly. Excessive analysis and the time taken to perform it and slow decision processes are the biggest problems for a program manager at any level trying to maintain cost, schedule and performance.

Mr. ROGERS. Your National Academies report talked about the need to clarify operational authorities for space. Can you expand on that? What is your view of unity of command versus unity of effort?

Mr. FAGA. Our concern was the delegation of authority to take action which is granted by the President to operational commanders. In the case of space, these delegations and rules of engagement are not well developed largely because such actions haven't been seriously contemplated until recently. While I think the most likely attacks would be cyber, jamming or laser, it is relevant to note that a direct ascent attack on a low orbit satellite requires only 13 minutes. A decision process that takes longer than that won't get the job done.

A related ongoing debate is whether the Commander of Stratcom should be empowered to direct the response of NRO satellites to attack or threat of it. I believe that even in time of conflict, that the DNI mechanisms for tasking and control of NRO assets should remain in place, albeit in tight coordination with the Stratcom Commander including appropriate participation in the JICSPOC. I lived a version of this problem while serving as DNRO during the First Gulf War. Control of certain assets was transferred from the multi-agency group that performed it for the DCI to DIA which wasn't trained in carrying it out. The result was a large drop in performance. Fortunately, there was time before combat operations began for DIA to get up to speed and perform well. Here, where timelines may be only minutes, changes from normal operating methods is likely to turn out badly.

Mr. ROGERS. Generally speaking, what authorities does the Director of the NRO have in terms of overall direction, budgeting, architecture development, operational direction, research and development, and acquisition approval? Is there any counterpart, in the military space program, that has the same authorities as the Director of the NRO? Would the military benefit from having someone with similar authorities?

Mr. FAGA. The DNRO has a substantial role in most of these areas but never complete. I'll answer individually to explain:

- The DNRO works for the SecDef and the DNI and exercises overall direction subject to their direction or approval. As a practical matter, direction from the SecDef and DNI is high level and the DNRO has substantial discretion to carry out that guidance within the NRO as she deems appropriate.
- The DNRO builds an NRO budget subject to annual guidance from the DNI and with a final budget approved by the DNI with concurrence from the DOD. The key here is that the number of people involved is relatively small compared to programs in DOD and the DNRO and her staff can interact with all of them.
- The DNRO is largely responsible for developing and maintaining a national reconnaissance architecture subject to the concurrence of the DNI and the DOD. She has considerable discretion here but not total control.
- The DNRO has little authority for operational control. The NRO launches and provides the ground station operating crew, maintains health of the satellite, etc. but all tasking comes through DNI mechanisms. Other than for engineering test, the DNRO issues no direction on the operational use of the NRO satellites.
- The Director has great discretion in the application of R&D funds. Typical of most companies, generally a % of the program is devoted to R&D with almost total discretion in how the funds are applied.
- Acquisition approval comes from the DNI with DOD concurrence (or the inverse for MIP funded activities). Once granted, the Director has substantial discretion in management of the program to its completion.

The person closest in authorities to the DNRO is the Commander, AF Space Command who has acquisition and also has operational authorities which the DNRO does not. He has a budgeting role but not one as strong as the DNRO. The Secretary of the Air Force has budgeting authority for about 90% of military space so these two executives have very significant roles.

Regarding establishing a "DNRO-like" person in DOD, I would note that, as described above, the DNRO has a powerful position but draws authorities and approvals from a range of seniors. The benefit she has is the ability to interact with relatively few people at senior levels and considerable discretion inside the NRO which is not typical in DOD. This speaks to my point in oral testimony about empowering the Program Manager where, in this case, the Program Manager is the DNRO. I think that is more important than a single person inserted in DOD somewhere to replicate the DNRO.

Mr. ROGERS. When you were the Director of the NRO, you also served as an Assistant Secretary of the Air Force. What are your thoughts on the importance of that the connection with the military and intelligence programs? What is the role of Principal DOD Space Advisor with regard to the NRO?

Mr. FAGA. It was helpful as it gave me a role within the AF that was useful, especially as the NRO hadn't been declassified and wasn't acknowledged. Perhaps more important was that I was a Presidential appointee, confirmed by the Senate. That increased standing in the Pentagon substantially. That said, I played a role in military space and NRO but didn't serve as a coordinator between them to any great extent.

I think the current arrangement, with the DNRO serving only in that capacity is the better arrangement as it is certainly a full time job.

I don't know the role of the PDSA in any detail, but believe that the role with regard to NRO is modest, one of achieving coordination and certainly cooperation but not direction.

Mr. ROGERS. What arrangements should be in place between the DOD and the IC and various commercial companies regarding the U.S. Government's ability to task and use commercial satellites in crisis or wartime?

Mr. FAGA. The DOD and IC do use commercial space companies extensively in peace, crisis and war. As long ago as the first Gulf War, at least half of satellite communications into theatre was provided by commercial providers. In more recent times, commercial imagery has also been used extensively in crisis and wartime situations.

I think that one thrust of your question is what can be expected of commercial providers in crisis and war. This is largely a matter of the contractual arrangement between the government and the provider. When I joined several company boards after service in government and a nonprofit, I quickly learned that risk is always monetized. So, if commercial service in conflict brings extra risk, it can be monetized through contract payments, provision of extra services and capabilities in the satellites, agreement by the government to provide certain protections, insurance and other means. The key is to anticipate and work out the expectations and contractual mechanisms in advance.

QUESTIONS SUBMITTED BY MR. COOPER

Mr. COOPER. This committee has focused on acquisition reform over the past two national defense authorization bills. Generally, how is acquisition within the space enterprise unique from the rest of DOD acquisition? More specifically, what areas of space acquisition require the most attention and are likely to require reforms specific to them?

Dr. HAMRE. Acquisition of space assets is not inherently different. But there are unique qualities to space that do impact acquisition. These are exceptionally expensive assets and we buy them in very limited numbers. This is more analogous to buying aircraft carriers than trucks. The long lead time and high expense requires a different oversight structure. But space acquisition is not inherently different from normal government acquisition. The broader question is could we use more commercial modalities to get space capabilities. Currently we focus on government-only spacecraft and these become exceptionally expensive and have very long development cycles. The commercial sector has much shorter cycles, which means cheaper satellites that are replaced more often as advanced technology becomes available. I believe we need to look at very different models for buying space-based capabilities.

Mr. COOPER. You noted that existing and emerging commercial capabilities represent opportunities for improving capacity and resilience, and that commercial space operations are particularly efficient. Could you elaborate on how using commercial capabilities, for example for imagery or space situational awareness, will help improve national security capability and capacity? And what lessons on efficiency can be learned and applied to enhance national security space operations?

Dr. HAMRE. There are a new generation of commercial satellite companies that are producing lower fidelity systems in great number. These are sometimes called cube-sats or micro-sats. The resolution will always be inferior because these are very small satellites (5 inch square and 20 inches long, for example) compared to current reconnaissance satellites that are enormous. So the images from these lower-fidelity satellites will not be useful for important intelligence missions. But they could be perfectly adequate for many military applications. The advantage of these small satellite constellations is that they are constantly improving the technology on the satellite, and can introduce these improvements every 6 months. Giant reconnaissance satellites freeze technology (remarkable technology, to be sure) for a 15 year period. Micro-sats are no substitute for our sophisticated satellites, but they are a very important potential complement, and could take on a much larger range of missions, especially for the Defense Department.

Mr. COOPER. This committee has focused on acquisition reform over the past two national defense authorization bills. Generally, how is acquisition within the space enterprise unique from the rest of DOD acquisition? More specifically, what areas of space acquisition require the most attention and are likely to require reforms specific to them?

Admiral ELLIS. There are many similarities between procurement of space systems and the acquisition of other DOD capabilities. There are also reasons why some of the policies, regulations and oversight are applicable to both.

There are some differences that should be considered, however. The first is the capability focus of our space systems. Past policies have focused on designing and building "exquisite" space systems where every ounce of capability and reliability has been designed in and little attention has been paid to resilience or robustness. This must change.

A second area is the long lifetime for which our on-orbit systems are designed. This has led to a post-launch technological status quo. Perhaps consideration of lower cost and shorter lifetimes is appropriate to allow technological refreshment at a faster rate. A second lifetime consideration could explore the possibility of modular on-orbit upgrades and refueling to provide the best of both worlds.

A third area for consideration is consistency of purpose and the sharing of best acquisition practices across the DOD, IC and commercial stove-pipes. There is an opportunity, without giving all space acquisition authority to a single entity, to more effectively share among all those contributing so much to national security space. Much good work is being done but it is not widely shared and its broader use has not been widely encouraged.

Mr. COOPER. This committee has focused on acquisition reform over the past two national defense authorization bills. Generally, how is acquisition within the space enterprise unique from the rest of DOD acquisition? More specifically, what areas of space acquisition require the most attention and are likely to require reforms specific to them?

Mr. FAGA. There are many similarities but the space enterprise tends to change at a higher pace. Planes, ships and tanks tend to have service lives of 20–40 years and more. While individual satellites may typically last 10–15 years, new requirements and technology tend to drive revised designs every few years. To do this well, all of the processes involved need to move faster than they do. Taking several years just to get to a decision of what to buy is way too long.

Space systems are largely information systems and much closer to terrestrial IT than to planes, ships and tanks. We need to recognize that most systems won't be built in large numbers or for long periods of time so don't need all of the "ilities" treatments that major defense systems receive. Like terrestrial IT, we need to think of services more than systems and provided by commercial providers under service contracts or with government-purchased satellites as appropriate. In either case, we need to think about the service we are obtaining rather than the platform and contract model we are using.

QUESTIONS SUBMITTED BY MR. LAMBORN

Mr. LAMBORN. Admiral Ellis' testimony was particularly strong in making the point that strategy must come first. What should our strategic vision for national security space be, and how can we ensure our strategy will function across the spectrum of conflict?

Dr. HAMRE. Our strategic vision for space must be integrated with our broad strategic vision for national security. Space needs to be able to make its contribution to our military success on earth. We must take steps to insure that we can reliably function through the spectrum of conflict conditions to support terrestrial military operations. Space will continue to be a critical capability, but we need reliability and resilience. Adversaries are now threatening our assured use of space, so we need to adapt our plans to insure that we can accomplish all our missions successfully. In some instances, this will place less dependence on space. It also means we need to change the way we approach space from a public standpoint. We are now able to draw on a much richer range of commercial assets, to include foreign commercial assets, for critical space functions. Drawing on a much wider range of assets will enhance deterrence and increase dissuasion of potential hostile actions.

Mr. LAMBORN. Please describe the importance of budget authority in DOD, and compare the budget authority that the Commander of Air Force Space Command has, in comparison to the Director of the NRO.

Dr. HAMRE. I need to make sure I properly understand this question. The Commander of the Air Force Space Command has budget authority for some things, such as operating his ground-based installations. But I assume that you are talking about the ability to buy satellites. I think there are three authorities that need to be balanced—the authority to establish requirements, the authority to buy things, and the authority to operate things. The NRO has the authority to buy things and operate things. The USAF Space Command largely has authority to set requirements and to operate things, but not to buy things. There is no easy answer on how to balance these three authorities. Organizations that establish requirements but don't have accountability for buying or operating things tends to lead to gold-plating of requirements and systems, for example. I would need to map out all the various authorities in order to properly answer your question.

Mr. LAMBORN. A review of the budget documents shows that the unclassified space RDT&E budgets are at a 30-year low. Why do you think that is?

Dr. HAMRE. I would need to study this carefully, and I have not. So my initial response is that we no longer need to spend so much money on unclassified space RDT&E because we now have such a robust private sector. 40 years ago, the Federal Government needed to invest in this, where today it can buy it from the private sector. And DOD continues to make significant investments in classified space RDT&E. But I do suspect that overall R&D spending on space by the federal government is down compared to years past. The more important question is how can we tap into the vitality I see in the private sector on space? That is the challenge of today.

Mr. LAMBORN. What should the future mission of the JICSpOC be? How does that compare to the current and future mission of the JSPOC?

Dr. HAMRE. Again, I don't know this to be the case, but I suspect that the JICSpOC is separate from JSPOC because non-defense agencies are wary of being sucked into a DOD-dominated environment. It is easier to get coordination if they are given a somewhat autonomous space separate from DOD. But I would need to study this problem more in order to give you a better answer.

Mr. LAMBORN. Admiral Ellis' testimony was particularly strong in making the point that strategy must come first. What should our strategic vision for national security space be, and how can we ensure our strategy will function across the spectrum of conflict?

Admiral ELLIS. As noted in the National Academy report provided to the Subcommittee, given the country's broad dependence on space for both civil and military activities, U.S. interests would appear to be served by a strategy focused on creating an environment in which there exist no means to unilaterally attack U.S. space systems without attribution and effective counters, or a future where space systems offer sufficient resiliency that such unilateral attacks are not effective in negating a space capability. However, given the dependence of potential adversaries on space systems in time of conflict, the interests of the United States may also be served by having the means to disable adversary space systems in time of crisis or conflict. Moreover, a number of means to attack space systems have been demonstrated or are postulated, and failure to protect against the use of such systems would put the United States at a significant disadvantage. While the United States may decide what space future it prefers, the United States is not the sole determiner of that future. U.S. actions will be constrained by what our potential adversaries—and even our friends—decide to do. Furthermore, frenetic innovation in the commercial space sector has the potential to be the main driver of change in the space domain. Put somewhat differently, the United States faces a short-term operational problem that needs to be addressed with urgency and it also faces a more complex, long-term strategic problem. In the short term, what should the United States do to counter the emerging, multi-faceted threat to U.S. national security space assets? Potential measures include hardening systems against known and predicted means of attack; establishing capabilities to mitigate the effects of successful attacks on U.S. space systems; expanding systems to detect attacks in progress, including confidently distinguishing attacks from other sources of failures; and reacting to them, implementing political-military means designed to deter attacks, and developing and deploying retaliatory systems and other means to hold adversaries' assets at risk. This is not just a matter of developing hardware; organizations, policies, doctrine, and operational concepts need to be modified or created in parallel. Policy issues include declaratory policies with regard to attacks on the national security space architecture, including commercial space systems that provide national security functions, as well as appropriate responses to attacks on significant commercial systems. Addressing this problem requires a clear understanding of the threat and the diverging time lines associated both with threat evolution and timely deployment of solutions.

Mr. LAMBORN. Your recent National Academies report talked about the need to clarify operational authorities for space. Can you please expand on that? What is your view of unity of command versus unity of effort? Who—if anyone—is respon- sible for disseminating information regarding warning and/or insight into adversarial operations across the defense and intelligence communities?

Admiral ELLIS. There have recently been some candid discussions about operational control of all national security satellites, including the NRO assets and those commercial communications satellites used for national security purposes, in the context of achieving consistent policies and clear, responsive decision-making in time of potential crisis. This is understandably, a complex technology, policy, and authority issue. In fairness, the discussion has arisen as a result of our appropriately re-defining the scope of "national security space" to include all of the space-borne resources we employ and those on which we rely as a nation and with our global partners. It should not and must not be viewed as a "power grab" but rather as an acknowledgement of newly appreciated realities of the nature, capabilities, and speed of potential threats.

This has resulted in the creation of the JICSPOC to simulate and evaluate potential challenges and solutions and to craft concepts of operation and clarify who does what and how in the event of attacks on U.S. satellites. In my view, that describes a place where a much-needed series of simulations and exercises can take place to enhance understanding of the national security space interrelationships, define overlapping capabilities and, most importantly, identify gaps in the structure, authority, and accountability. I fully support such immediate interagency efforts; they are long overdue.

On the other hand, I believe strongly in unity of command, authority and accountability. As I note often, collaboration is not the same as consensus; someone has to be in charge. This is particularly true in the national security space domain where challenges can manifest themselves quickly, sometimes at the speed of light. The precise organizational and authority structure should be left to the agencies involved and not imposed by fiat or decree from external entities.

I support the experimental character of the JICSPOC but agree that the lessons from its tests need to move quickly to a single command center, appropriately staffed by all stakeholders, with a clearly defined chain of command. They are not lessons learned just because we write them down; we actually have to learn them and things need to change as a result.

Mr. LAMBORN. Please describe the importance of budget authority in DOD, and compare the budget authority that the Commander of Air Force Space Command has, in comparison to the Director of the NRO.

Admiral ELLIS. As the Subcommittee is well aware, budget authority is the final arbiter of influence in the DOD, just as it is in any organization. From a procurement perspective, Air Force Space Command executes much of its authority through the Space and Missile Systems Center (SMC) at Los Angeles AFB, California, which designs and acquires all Air Force and most Department of Defense space systems. As with all DOD procurement, these processes are subject to procurement regulations and policies that may not be specifically designed to support the unique character of the space enterprise.

I cannot compare the NRO's budget authority but sense that it is adequate to their needs and that they operate under a much more streamlined and tightly-coupled process.

Mr. LAMBORN. A review of the budget documents shows that the unclassified space RDT&E budgets are at a 30-year low. Why do you think that is?

Admiral ELLIS. In my opinion, the decline in Federal space R&D spending is simply a result of the budget pressures on discretionary spending forcing choices between development and procurement.

From a private sector perspective, many worthy research projects are risky, with uncertain prospects for success or future utility, and may require a long-term commitment of resources and infrastructure. These qualities of the science enterprise lead to underinvestment by private industry, which in general is more focused on lower-risk research and product development with the promise of short-term results. This is why industry spends 80 cents of every R&D dollar on development, and only 20 cents on basic and applied research (for civilian science agencies, the ratio is reversed).

Mr. LAMBORN. What should the future mission of the JICSpOC be? How does that compare to the current and future mission of the JSPOC?

Admiral ELLIS. The stated purpose of the newly-created JICSPOC is for the military, Intelligence Community (IC), and commercial partners to craft concepts of operation and clarify who does what and how in the event of attacks on U.S. satellites. In my view, that describes a place where a much-needed series of simulations and exercises can take place to enhance understanding of the national security space interrelationships, define overlapping capabilities and, most importantly, identify gaps in the structure, authority, and accountability. I fully support such immediate interagency and commercial outreach efforts; they are long overdue.

On the other hand, I believe strongly in unity of command, authority and accountability. As I note often, collaboration is not the same as consensus; someone has to be in charge. This is particularly true in the national security space domain where challenges can manifest themselves quickly, sometimes at the speed of light.

I support the experimental character of the JICSPOC but agree that the lessons from its tests need to move quickly to a single command center, appropriately staffed by all stakeholders, with a clearly defined chain of command. They are not lessons learned just because we write them down; we actually have to learn them and things need to change as a result.

Mr. LAMBORN. Admiral Ellis' testimony was particularly strong in making the point that strategy must come first. What should our strategic vision for national security space be, and how can we ensure our strategy will function across the spectrum of conflict?

Mr. FAGA. Strategy is the first and topmost of the steps leading to actions. It sets the overall goals and plans. The trouble with most strategies is that they are aspirational, not realistic and fail to become true guides for action. The strategy challenge for space now is the need to shift from information satellites living in a benign environment to systems that have to survive in conflict. The strategy begins with laying out what the expectations of commanders are as well as an understanding from providers of what can realistically be achieved. Strategies that simply state, "systems will be made resilient" are not useful statements.

Mr. LAMBORN. Your recent National Academies report talked about the need to clarify operational authorities for space. Can you please expand on that? What is your view of unity of command versus unity of effort? Who—if anyone—is responsible for disseminating information regarding warning and/or insight into adversarial operations across the defense and intelligence communities?

Mr. FAGA. In partial response, please see my answer to question 21. Unity of command vs unity of effort in this context refers to whether DOD controls NRO satellites, at least for purposes of protection, in time of crisis or war. I recommend the unity of effort approach where the NRO continues to respond to DNI direction in the use of its satellites. One of the lessons to me while serving as DNRO during the first Gulf War was that DOD is not the only user of satellite reconnaissance during the fight. The NSC, State and others had pressing needs which were largely adjudicated by the DCI and now the DNI. Even regarding protection, I can envision a situation where DOD says you need to move or you'll be killed in a few minutes, and the DNI saying the info being gained at this moment is so important that it's worth that price. Moreover, I think this is an issue debated over the least likely threat-direct attack. Cyber, jamming and laser threats are far more likely in my estimation.

Regarding the dissemination of warning and insight, both the IC and DOD communities do this. Typically, the IC is collecting longer term and more detailed information like "what are the specific capabilities of this threat" while the DOD is providing warning near the moment of attack.

Mr. LAMBORN. Please describe the importance of budget authority in DOD, and compare the budget authority that the Commander of Air Force Space Command has, in comparison to the Director of the NRO.

Mr. FAGA. I believe that their budget authority is similar but their ability to influence what budget authority they receive is quite different. Regarding similar authority, both must receive their budgets pursuant to a budget submission by the President and Congressional Authorization and Appropriation. Both receive funds subject to the limitations of the Program Elements used and to reprogramming rules and thresholds. However, the reporting chain of the DNRO is far shorter and she has the ability to directly engage the Principals who decide her budget. Both the DNRO and Commander AFSPC are subject to the effects of budget drills that suddenly move significant money from their program to another. However, the entire National Intel Program is 10% of the size of the Defense budget and the likelihood of an event of which affects the NRO of which the DNRO is unaware, is far smaller than for the Commander AFSPC.

Mr. LAMBORN. A review of the budget documents shows that the unclassified space RDT&E budgets are at a 30-year low. Why do you think that is?

Mr. FAGA. I think there are two elements to this decline: reduced spending for research on new technologies or systems and reduced spending on new starts. Regarding the first, the temptation in tight budget times is to push off the future to maintain present capability. Similarly, the desire for continued service from legacy systems tends to push out spending for new starts. Existing systems have many supporters among current users; new ideas have few supporters and are consequently very hard to get funded in the President's Budget.

Congressional interest in this matter is particularly important, because it is often the Congress that pushes the Administration to take on new things. In intelligence, it is important to keep developing new capabilities that adversaries will be unaware of for some period of time. Those are the most valuable capabilities.

Mr. LAMBORN. What should the future mission of the JICSpOC be? How does that compare to the current and future mission of the JSPOC?

Mr. FAGA. The JICSpOC should become the ops center for the era we are entering where space systems are subject to interference or attack. I see it subsuming and replacing the JSPOC. The JICSpOC is learning how to operate on timelines measured in minutes while the JSPOC operates on timelines measured in hours to days. Lt. Gen. Raymond once described the JSPOC as largely a space cataloging operation. The JICSpOC will need to become a combat operations center.

QUESTIONS SUBMITTED BY MR. COFFMAN

Mr. COFFMAN. The current acquisition approach can take 10-plus years to deliver a new capability. This approach cannot keep pace with the evolving threat and advances in technology. What changes to the acquisition process will need to happen in order to reduce the time to deliver new capability to less than 5 years?

Dr. HAMRE. This problem is not unique to space. In general, defense acquisition has evolved to take long times. The barrier to get new programs is so high that the Services often load up the requirements for the program, thinking that it is their only chance. So we postulate capabilities that technology cannot currently provide for some systems and develop that technology along the way. I personally would favor an acquisition system that allows incremental advances over time. We have done that in the past very successfully, for example with the F–16. But we have not done that with space procurement. This is largely because the number of units we buy is very small and over a long period of time. So we tend to load them up with capabilities that are very advanced and do have technical uncertainty. This is one of the reasons why I favor relying much more on commercially-provided capability, which is expanding.

Mr. COFFMAN. Where are the key areas that you see commercial capability most effectively augmenting the national security space mission, both from a capability and a space resiliency perspective?

Dr. HAMRE. Right now I think the strongest area is in communications capabilities. But I think we will increasingly see much stronger commercial capabilities for reconnaissance and surveillance. The fidelity will lag our government satellites, but commercial fidelity is getting very good. For precision navigation, it is more a case of using the positioning signals from satellites of other countries. We are seeing growing commercial capabilities for space launch, and that will continue. All together, these commercial developments give us the promise of more redundancy and reconstitutability. But we need to change how we think about buying space capabilities if we are going to take advantage of these trends.

Mr. COFFMAN. The NRO has seen some real success through the application of autonomy and analytics capabilities into their architecture—driving down costs and improving the intelligence value and responsiveness of their enterprise. What other space-based missions (beyond intelligence), could benefit from the application of advanced analytic capabilities?

Dr. HAMRE. I must plead insufficient knowledge to properly answer your question. I don't know enough about how the NRO has accomplished this in order to postulate other options we might pursue.

Mr. COFFMAN. Each space protection program is contained within its own Special Access Program (SAP) with a limited number of billets, creating knowledge silos. How should DOD and the Intelligence Community balance security concerns with their ability to leverage technology and capabilities across the government and industry?

Dr. HAMRE. You have hit on a key problem. By definition, very few people know about the details of SAP programs, and for good reason. But this also means we never can build on the advances of one program to make another SAP program more effective and less expensive. The mechanisms of coordination for SAP programs are largely administrative, rather than programmatic. It would be an interesting experiment to create a small cell reporting directly to the Deputy Secretary of Defense, charged with the goal of seeing where the program details of one SAP program might be usefully applied to another SAP program.

Mr. COFFMAN. The current acquisition approach can take 10-plus years to deliver a new capability. This approach cannot keep pace with the evolving threat and advances in technology. What changes to the acquisition process will need to happen in order to reduce the time to deliver new capability to less than 5 years?

Admiral ELLIS. There are some dramatically different approaches that should be considered as we address the rapid technological change and growing threats that confront us.

The first is the capability focus of our space systems. Past policies have focused on designing and building "exquisite" space systems where every ounce of capability and reliability has been designed in and little attention has been paid to resilience or robustness. This must change.

A second area is the long lifetime for which our on-orbit systems are designed. This has led to a post-launch technological status quo. Perhaps consideration of lower cost and shorter lifetimes is appropriate to allow technological refreshment at a faster rate. A second lifetime consideration could explore the possibility of modular on-orbit upgrades and refueling to provide the best of both worlds.

A third area for consideration is consistency of purpose and the sharing of best acquisition practices across the DOD, IC and commercial stove-pipes. There is an opportunity, without giving all space acquisition authority to a single entity, to more effectively share insights among all those contributing so much to national security space. Much good work is being done but it is not widely shared and its broader use has not been widely encouraged. Here, a single DOD-level Undersecretary for Space would have a key role.

Mr. COFFMAN. Where are the key areas that you see commercial capability most effectively augmenting the national security space mission, both from a capability and a space resiliency perspective?

Admiral ELLIS. Commercial contributors are already making key contributions across the full spectrum of national security space. In addition to the long-standing contributions to our multi-frequency, space-borne communications architecture, we now see opportunities emerging in commercial imagery, earth-sensing using other sensors, and, of course, the developing launch systems. All of these can bring enhanced capability, multi-nodal redundancy, and enhanced resiliency.

A key element of our ability to capitalize on commercial space is resisting the temptation to over-control and over-regulate. We are still not buying commercial SATCOM capacity as efficiently as we might and spectrum control and allocation processes are highly bureaucratic. We cannot approach the commercial sector with the same slow processes and restrictive regulation and expect to get a different outcome.

Mr. COFFMAN. The NRO has seen some real success through the application of autonomy and analytics capabilities into their architecture—driving down costs and improving the intelligence value and responsiveness of their enterprise. What other space-based missions (beyond intelligence), could benefit from the application of advanced analytic capabilities?

Admiral ELLIS. As I described above, while R&D investment is essential, so is the ability to know where the need is largest and the potential positive impact the greatest. This is a perfect place for real, even-handed, and dispassionate analytical capabilities. We need more effective tools for system-wide analysis to ensure we are focusing on what is most important. While allocation of funds is sometimes a valuable metric, it cannot define where resources can be most effectively employed. The "critical infrastructure in space" that we have created must be carefully analyzed to ensure that we really understand the capability and resiliency challenges confronting us and that we are not making decisions on the basis of assumptions that are no longer valid as a result of dramatic changes in the technology, organizational structures, or the operating environment.

Mr. COFFMAN. Each space protection program is contained within its own Special Access Program (SAP) with a limited number of billets, creating knowledge silos. How should DOD and the Intelligence Community balance security concerns with their ability to leverage technology and capabilities across the government and industry?

Admiral ELLIS. Unfortunately, the plethora of national security leaks and revelations over the last five years, from Snowden to WikiLeaks, has brought reconsideration of the movement toward more information and intelligence sharing that began in the days after 9/11. There are legitimate concerns, as we see Top Secret documents appearing in the public domain, that higher levels of classification and limited access are key elements in preserving the classified character of our most precious technologies.

In my opinion, retaining the balance inferred in the question is appropriate but is getting more difficult each day. One technique is to carefully parse programs into distinct sub-elements, including basic technology, system integration and operational concepts, that can be appropriately shared but do not reveal the entirety of the program and its impact.

A second approach is to allow DOD to develop and provide "black box" capabilities to civilian or non-DOD space programs that are bolt-on, tamper-proof and add capabilities without revealing the classified technologies or operational concepts. If we are to get full use of all space assets, effectively integrate them into a security network, and create a more resilient system across the DOD, IC, and commercial sectors, everyone must be included and contribute.

Mr. COFFMAN. The current acquisition approach can take 10-plus years to deliver a new capability. This approach cannot keep pace with the evolving threat and advances in technology. What changes to the acquisition process will need to happen in order to reduce the time to deliver new capability to less than 5 years?

Mr. FAGA. As a baseline, I noted in my testimony that several decades ago the standard planning number for a new satellite acquisition was 42 months. This number assumed that the technology was ready and development could begin. This target was usually met. Commercial satellite procurements today usually meet this timeline or do better. Acquisitions in 24–36 months are common.

Today's military and IC satellite systems are more complex but available technology is also more mature. The big change is the amount of time deciding and agreeing on what to build as well as the contracting process before real development work begins. This can easily consume 3 to 5 years and partially explains the 5 to 10 year gap that you point out.

Another delaying factor is the annual budget process that allows everyone not in favor of the program to have an annual opportunity to delay, underfund or even cancel it. These budget drills often put programs into an undesirable or even unworkable funding profile that further delays development and adds greatly to total cost. As these processes are much less at work in SAP programs, they tend to do better in terms of cost and schedule.

One approach is to reverse the impediments described above. Another is to do more buying of a service or a turn-key system where the government specifies what it wants at the beginning and takes delivery at the end. So, in the case of commercial imagery, NGA buys imagery from Digital Globe generally independent of which of several satellites does the collection. However, the government could also turn to satellite builders for complete satellites delivered on orbit. Commercial imagery and satcom companies generally use this approach.

An approach resembling this was used in the 90s and was called Total System Procurement Responsibility (TSPR) which largely failed. However, it didn't fail because the concept was flawed but because it's implementation was flawed. The approach still requires government involvement but government managers thought it meant "hands off." There needs to be customer involvement throughout but it is largely not directive in nature, it serves to help with modification of requirements, choosing among alternatives when problems arise and other major issues. However, it is not involved in the minutia of the problem.

Mr. COFFMAN. Where are the key areas that you see commercial capability most effectively augmenting the national security space mission, both from a capability and a space resiliency perspective?

Mr. FAGA. Commercial satcom has long been a major supplier of service to national security space. The DOD CIO has recently estimated that 40% of DOD satcom is commercial. I recall that during the first Gulf War it was estimated at 60%. Nonetheless, I believe that there will likely always be a need for specialized, highly resilient satcom systems built for and operated by DOD. However, in many cases it would be possible to purchase the satellite under a commercial-like contract where the government specifies at the beginning and takes over the system on orbit. This can work for complicated satellites but only for those that can be fully specified at the beginning of the program. This is not practical where there is substantial development and non-recurring engineering involved.

The national space community has used commercial satellite imagery for over 20 years with good success. As offerings increase, this usage will surely increase as well. As a result, the NRO and NGA have set up a special combined office to deal with the blending of commercial and NRO systems that is clearly coming.

It is possible that commercial PNT, weather and space situational awareness offerings will be available in the near future.

A particularly attractive approach to use of commercial satellites is for hosted payloads that are no acknowledged. The most valuable capability is one not known to others. Such a secret is hard to keep today but SAP programs succeed at doing so routinely.

Mr. COFFMAN. The NRO has seen some real success through the application of autonomy and analytics capabilities into their architecture—driving down costs and improving the intelligence value and responsiveness of their enterprise. What other space-based missions (beyond intelligence), could benefit from the application of advanced analytic capabilities?

Mr. FAGA. I am not familiar with these efforts in any detail. I know that the NRO has been using autonomous means to quickly review data in order to sort from a large volume of data to smaller amounts that analysts can quickly exploit. Other IC agencies are also doing this on other forms of data. Some of these efforts seek to exploit different sources of data at the machine level and do valuable sorting and combining of data before presentation to the analyst so that the material that is presented is more comprehensive and valuable. It is estimated that analysts spend about 60% of their time searching for and organizing data and only 40% analyzing. Clearly, managers want to reduce that 60% substantially and increase the time for value-added work.

Another application of analytics becoming important in the development of space systems and others, it model based systems engineering. In this technique, a computer model of the entire system is developed which provides greater insight into the system than previous methods and allows for easy examination of potential changes to the system. Many NRO contractors are now using this technique.

Mr. COFFMAN. Each space protection program is contained within its own Special Access Program (SAP) with a limited number of billets, creating knowledge silos. How should DOD and the Intelligence Community balance security concerns with their ability to leverage technology and capabilities across the government and industry?

Mr. FAGA. SAP programs are valuable because they successfully maintain secrecy for very long periods such as the entire development period for a new capability. Often, knowledge of the very existence of a vulnerability being exploited by a SAP program, or knowledge of the existence of the SAP program even absent any details, is enough to make it worthless. In such cases, very tight security is clearly necessary.

There are two problems with SAP programs of which I am aware: 1. Once a program is put into SAP status, the security program is developed by the Program Manager. This means that there is little consistency among the various SAP programs. While I am in favor of the very strict security programs used, they should be consistent among them. 2. The highly classified nature of SAPs and exacerbated by the point above, it is often very hard to provide the capability to legitimate users, be they intel analysts or combat commanders. In the case of the combat commander, for example, it is vital that the capability be understood, practiced with and accessible in a combat situation. This is often not the case. The key question is whether this magnificent technical capability is able to offer operational value. I have seen war-game situations where an important SAP capability wasn't available to a combatant commander because the command and control link was knocked out but the system itself remained functional.